THE
GUELPH
PAPERS

editor
Robert F. Nixon

associate editor
Allen Linden

Peter Martin Associates Limited

Peter Martin Associates Limited
17 Inkerman Street, Toronto 5, Ontario

Contents

Preface

A political party exists because it is dedicated to certain principles of
public policy. On the foundation of these principles, parties forge
their platforms. Periodically these platforms are placed before the
people, at which time they can vote for them or reject them.

The Liberal Party in Ontario has a long and distinguished record
of service to the people of Ontario—both in government and in opposition. It has (and has always had) a philosophy and a program based
upon it. Nevertheless, as we approach the new decade of the 1970s, I
think it is appropriate to reassess the Liberal philosophy and, if
necessary, to set out in a new direction.

In the Liberal Party, this is a democratic process. In January of
1969, in order to begin the reassessment, I asked Professor Allen M.
Linden of the Osgoode Hall Law School of York University to bring
together for consultation with my caucus, my party and myself the
leading experts of our province. On August 22-24, 1969 at the University of Guelph, the policy dialogue involving over four hundred of the
party rank and file and the experts began. The first caucus conference
had been held in Peterborough at Trent University in September of
1968 and dealt largely with organizational matters. This book contains some of the papers that were presented at the Guelph Conference, some of the comments made on papers and some other material.
Many excellent papers could not be included because of space and
time constraints. This book has been produced so that the public will
be able to study them. The views expressed are not the Liberal Party
platform. This will be hammered out over the next year or so. First,
the various riding associations will debate the views outlined here.
Regional meetings will then be held. The process will culminate in a
policy rally in 1971, at which time our platform will be finalized.

I am adamant that our campaign in 1971 will be based on a full
policy statement that will be a blueprint for a new Liberal government. This blueprint for modern government must be and will be

arrived at democratically. I know that the people of this province will respond to policies which deal openly and hard-headedly with the hopes and problems of the community on an informed, realistic basis.

All of us are committed to the truth and strength of the democratic process. This means not only the right of the majority to rule, but the responsibility of the people to see that their views are reflected in the political processes of the system. Since all citizens are not equally concerned, it is for us party members—Liberal Party members—to see that our party is responsible to the people and responsive to the needs of the community. This has been largely accomplished by our constitution's emphasis on accountability. It must be our goal to do the same for a Liberal legislature and a Liberal government in this province.

I consider it my responsibility as leader, however, to speak out frankly and firmly in those areas where our citizens must know my stand. It would be impossible for all my views to coincide precisely with those of every member of the party. I know this is understood and appreciated, which is why communication from you to members of the caucus is such an important part in our everyday handling of our job.

I want to make it clear that the responsibility for our political fortune is mine, and I must be the judge of how general policy decision, accepted by the Party, becomes a part of our Liberal program. However, the decisions of the Party, as outlined in our constitution, are the operative decisions. We believe in the widest possible involvement of citizens and taxpayers in our efforts and that these members have responsibilities and privileges that are respected, responsibilities to support the Party and work for it, and the privilege of taking part in policy development and in representing the Party. Our constitution, which I support wholeheartedly, requires leadership review periodically, at which time members should speak out about my role and how it can be changed and improved. I know we are united; we share a common cause and common principles, and because of this we will move forward to win a great victory in this province.

I want to express my appreciation to the committee, under the chairmanship of Professor Allen Linden, which undertook the planning and preparation of the Guelph Conference. Mr. Tim Reid, the caucus member responsible to the committee, worked long and effectively this past summer, with the help of Robin Russell in my office, to see that our time was put to good use. And more than anything else, we are deeply indebted to those people in the community, who are not necessarily members of the Party, but who wrote papers and put forward their own ideas for our discussion and who attended various sections of the Conference to assist us. I am grateful to my caucus which was so active in all the planning and deliberations at Guelph. The young rapporteurs, assembled by Peter Huntley, and the discussion leaders added greatly to the excitement and value of the conference. I am lastly indebted to Karin Stephen, Sandy Noble and Yvonne Ferguson for their help in the preparation of the manuscript.

Robert F. Nixon
January, 1970

1

A New Direction for Ontario
Robert F. Nixon

There is a certain restlessness abroad in the world. Students are riot-
ing in Montreal, Germany, Paris, Washington. Black people, Indians
and poor people are demanding equality. Labour unions, through
strikes, are seeking a better deal for their membership. Farmers are
discontented and have even taken to the highways on their tractors
to protest. And French-speaking Canadians have shown that they are
not contented with the status quo in Canada. These problems are
symptomatic of a yearning for the same thing—a new direction for
our society. I believe that it is time for a new government in Ontario
that is committed to moving us in a new direction.

As Canadians abandon their home towns and move to the cities
in search of opportunity, they often leave behind their roots, their
identity, their religion. Families begin to lose their influence as stabil-
izers of the young. For many (the educated, the diligent, the lucky)
it is an exhilarating experience as they make their work in their
adopted communities. But for many others (the under-educated, the
not-so-diligent, the unlucky) the experience is a debilitating one. The
loneliness of a large city, where success is measured largely in economic terms, where neighbours often do not know one another, and
where too many people perform dull, meaningless tasks in dreary
surroundings, oppresses and stifles them. And in order to harness the
great technological achievements of modern science, man has had to
create large-scale organisations. These massive corporations, universities, unions, governments have enabled mankind to combat disease,
famine and depression, to smash the atom and to explore space. But
these vast institutions somehow seem to have got out of our control,
which has led men to feel powerless, insignificant, helpless and even
hopeless. Many become alienated from society, they stop caring
about their country, their community, their family, their job. And
this feeling of alienation has affected too many of our young people,
who should not be thus affected. Too many turn away from estab-

1

lished patterns of life to commit crimes. (Although young people between sixteen and twenty-four years make up only 10 percent of our population, they account for over one-half the indictable crimes committed). A few "tune in", "turn on" and "drop out". Others lend their efforts to various protest movements like Vietnam, separatism, student power, seeking in some small way to express themselves in a society that does not seem to care about them.

It is not that I am against protest. Indeed, there is much to protest against when thousands of Canadians live in poverty as the rest of us grow rich, when nations stand poised to annihilate one another, when our lakes and rivers are heedlessly polluted, when thousands are needlessly slaughtered on our highways each year, when Indians, Eskimos and other minority groups are discriminated against. But dissent that consists only of such sporadic efforts as a protest march or a sit-in, sustained neither by hard work nor reason, is not very helpful. That kind of lazy and irresponsible protest—which seeks to destroy without being prepared to rebuild—is mere self-indulgence.

I prefer the kind of criticism that, in addition to pointing out problems, offers responsible solutions, not quick and easy ones, for there are no such solutions to the agonizing problems besetting our country. And I prefer those who are prepared to devote their time and effort on a continuing basis to the task of reshaping our society in the years ahead.

But we cannot return to the halcyon days of a century ago, appealing as that prospect may be. We must remake our present institutions, both governmental and private, to enable individuals to express themselves, to have some impact on their surroundings, to become involved in the shaping of their own destinies. We must build a society that permits each individual to develop to his full potential. We must ensure a decent standard of living in pleasant surroundings for all the people of Ontario. Our mass organizations must be rendered responsive to the needs of the individuals they are supposed to serve, instead of making individuals subservient to the needs of the organization. We must make individual Canadians, and our young people particularly, feel that they *can* make a difference, that they *do* matter, that they are *not* irrelevant.

But is liberalism up to the task? I believe that the principles of liberalism are as relevant today as they ever were, and we are dedicated to those principles. Our party's purpose is to put these principles into

2

effect. For a party that does not stand for principle is no party at all.

The root of the liberal philosophy remains today as it has always been—a passionate dedication to the freedom of the individual. But the liberal does much more than espouse this freedom: he strives continually to expand the amount of individual freedom in society. In other words, he works to liberate as many individuals from the confining influences of poverty, ignorance, background, geography and nature. The liberal, therefore, is a *liberator* (the very word comes from the latin verb to liberate); he is not the liberated person. Hence the ever-present concern with reform, human betterment and progress in the hearts of liberals everywhere. Almost instinctively the liberal approaches issues and problems with the questions, What are the weak points of this or that program? How can we improve the present situation? What is the best machinery to utilize? The conservative, as I understand, instinctively reacts by defending the status quo, demanding clear proof of the need for change and then reforming to the smallest degree necessary to remedy the problem.

This, then, is the essence of liberalism—the perpetual pressing forward to a freer society where individuals can develop to their full potential, a continual removing of barriers blocking the avenues of individual progress. The reason for this passion is the realization that the best society can be achieved only through the individual efforts of all our people. The task of the liberal is to fight for this elusive goal—a society where every individual will have an equal opportunity to learn, to work, to strive, to grow, to achieve, and to succeed. This does not mean, of course, that every individual will be equal or will secure an equal share of the fruits of society. People have always been, and will continue to be, unequal in ability and diligence. Their rewards will therefore differ and should differ—but until each person has an equal opportunity to succeed, our society will have need of liberals.

From what I gather, conservatism prizes freedom of the individual as well as does liberalism. My impression, however, is that conservatives are more concerned with *potential freedom* than with the *real freedom* which liberals strive towards. One cannot have real freedom unless the conditions within society permit each individual actually to exercise his freedom. The difference is between *freedom in theory* and *freedom in fact.* It is the latter which liberals wish to create. For example, a man has the freedom to choose a doctor if he is ill and to

3

select a lawyer if he is in trouble. But this is only a theoretical freedom if he has no money to pay the doctor or lawyer. Potentially anyone can become the prime minister of Canada, or the president of the CBC, the CNR, GM or GE, but liberals know that this is not a real freedom unless a person has been properly educated and has the right family background. Liberals want to change this potential freedom into real freedom and to do this they wish to liberate people from their ignorance by providing equal educational opportunity.

To provide this atmosphere of freedom, liberals are prepared to utilize government actively. They view government as an instrument to be used for human betterment. It is not the enemy of the people but their servant, and they should use it willingly. Conservatives tend to avoid governmental action, preferring solutions to problems by non-governmental intervention. Conservatives seem to prefer reluctant government, whereas liberals advocate more involved government.

Liberals are more prepared to sacrifice economic freedoms to provide wider personal freedom. Property rights, while they are respected by liberals, are revered by conservatives. This is the battle raging in the American South where, to supply to negroes personal freedom, property rights are being interfered with. Liberals believe that often those who cry out for economic freedom are really only disguising their lack of devotion to individual freedom. To liberals, where the two conflict the choice is easy. Economic freedom yields to the superior claim of individual freedom.

You may not know that the Liberal Party in Ontario rededicated itself to the philosophy of liberalism in 1964. It enshrined in its new provincial constitution, after some heated discussion, as its first object, "to advocate and support liberal political principles". Thus, the Liberal Party in Ontario has given primacy in its objectives to the promotion and support of a political philosophy, thereby accepting the idea that the role of political parties is to transmute political principles into governmental action.

The machinery of the Legislature and the government itself would be a Liberal government's first area of reform. The irrelevancy of a silent, non-participating body of backbenchers supporting an administration that is independent and all-powerful is obvious. The role of the Opposition itself is difficult to make meaningful when no workable committee system or powers of investigation are available. Even the size of the administration, with twenty-three cabinet ministers and

4

the same stereotyped portfolio divisions, must be reformed.

It is my goal to make the Liberal Party in the province, and a Liberal government in Queen's Park, respond to the full potential of the individual and to see that the right of self-realization through community service is a part of modern government.

Underlying this is the need to provide a basic level of life for all our citizens, who must be assured that in our land no one goes without proper food, housing, medical care, education and opportunity to show personal initiative.

There is no doubt that the guaranteed minimum income administered by a negative income tax is the best approach to this matter, but one which should be regarded as a national goal in the interests of Canadians as individuals and the unity of our country.

But even a guaranteed annual income will not solve all our poverty problems, for poverty is more than just an absence of income: it is a state of mind, a state of spirit. To uplift a man's spirit is a far more difficult task than to raise his income. We must begin to provide marketable skills to those of our poor who can be taught them. We must, if necessary, be prepared to move people who wish to move across the province to places where job opportunities exist. We must make an inventory of the skills we shall require in the years ahead, encourage people to train men for these jobs, and dissuade them from learning to perform jobs that are destined for extinction. The path of the future in combating poverty, therefore, is to be more selective and specialized, to choose target areas for attention and to exert our-. selves to a greater extent. Only then can we hope to obliterate poverty in this wealthy province.

A direct extension of this principle of individual worth must be our attitude towards the rights of individuals to operate their affairs in smaller local groups and to have the right of full consultation before these arrangements are changed. The Conservative tendency to centralize authority is against the current of development which must emphasize community autonomy and the spirit of initiative and experimentation. Modern technology and communication now gives us an opportunity to stress local autonomy, and it is around this cornerstone that I want our discussions on municipal affairs and tax policy to be based.

The whole question of tax reform is an increasingly vital matter. This follows not only from escalating rates, but the continuing stand-off among the three levels of government over sharing or division of tax responsibilities. The avowed policy of the Conservative government in this province to impose a separate income tax within the next two years is the setting in which we can continue our own review of policy. I believe that a political promise to reduce the rate of public cost expansion is not irresponsible, but it must be made only after careful investigation. I am convinced that new initiatives and a fresh approach by a Liberal government in this province can carry out economies to the benefit of our people. I know that the future of our nation is best served by cooperative problem solving among the three levels of government, rather than the political infighting that has harmed our confederation and is certainly costing us money, particularly in the relationship between the province and the municipalities.

Economic development of Ontario, and particularly equalization of opportunity, considering the northern and eastern parts of the province, must be an important political concern. I believe in a program for Ontario which contains the principles of the Canada Development Corporation accepted by our party. I want our people in Ontario to have an opportunity to invest in our resources and to have a channel for our savings to be operative in the expansion of our economy and to improve the level of Canadian control. Provincial development bonds sold for this purpose would provide a vehicle that would be fair, manageable, and have far-reaching advantages for our people.

The use of provincial development bonds will work well in Ontario; better than at the federal level. Our natural resources will attract investment from our own citizens, giving a real alternative to the money drain away from Ontario into the New York market. We can gather the capital that will accelerate economic development of the North and at the same time have a powerful level to strengthen Canadian ownership and management.

The economic future of Ontario is most promising. The advantages we have over competitors in the United States and our tremendous geographic location, coupled with the resources that are ours, are an exciting prospect, particularly if government policy can assist in their development from the standpoint of conservation, equalization of opportunity, and expanding employment prospects.

We are entering a new world in every sense. For two thousand

6

years our conscience has driven us to react to the miseries of our fellow man while concentrating on our own prospects. The most convenient salve was that, in fact, nothing in the knowledge of man could change the situation. This is being swept aside, not only by technology, but by the human spirit. Farmers can now feed the world. Doctors can now cure disease. Financiers can now industrialize. Technology can revolutionize the standard of living for all.

We must realize that within the next thirty years our responsibility as individuals to our fellow man will be paramount. While the idealistic goals of the past will be achieved, government and taxpayers will provide a solid standard of living for everyone; education priorities will move dramatically towards the development of individuals rather than the manufacture of professionals; the challenge of initiating environment improvements to cope with the ravages of economic growth will be met in large scale; and the provision of parks and recreational facilities, and the strengthening of wilderness reserves will overcome crass objectives.

If we as Liberals can bring about these changes, it will not be as previous administrations have tried to do by simply coping, effectively or otherwise, with the province's crises as they arrive day by day. I want a program that deals with these goals; I want to lead the discussions that develop the program; and I want to put the program before the thinking citizens of this province, the citizens who pay the bills and who live in the ommunities. We will have this program, and we will win the confidence of the people to implement it.

As Liberals on the provincial level, we shall continue to exert our independence in policy matters. We have a responsibility to cooperate with the federal party on national goals as they apply here. This must include the recognition and expansion of language rights and support for programs designed to accomplish equality of opportunity across Canada, such as medicare and education.

We must establish a province of creative diversity, where experiment is not discouraged but invited, a province where variety is fostered not inhibited, a province where the spirit of freedom thrives. The citizens of Ontario must believe that we are the masters of our destiny, that we *are* more than grains of sand being blown about on an endless beach. Only then will we be able to say that we have set out on a new direction for Ontario.

2

Learning in the Age of Wonder
Lloyd Dennis

ONTARIO, JUNE, 2000 A.D.

Neil Alexander Ellis, one of 35 million Canadians sharing the dawn of a new century, has just negotiated a contract that describes his professional responsibility as environmental engineer.* But Neil Alexander Ellis is more than that. Now in his early twenties, he was born when the moon and Mars had already been conquered by man. The Dawn of the Space Age, some called it. The Age of the Astronaut, the Golden Age of Space Travel, the age when man's sophisticated science launched him paradoxically beyond his earthly cocoon and into an era of renewed contemplation—the Age of Wonder.

Neil barely escaped the Age of the Institution, that twentieth century period when his forbears herded together—or allowed themselves to be herded—under the banners of expediency, efficiency, custom and conformity. It was the time of Organization Man, when goods were processed and people programmed; the golden harvest of the affluent state was offered to those who could reap it, and Ontario proudly won the title, "Province of Opportunity".

And this was the path of progress that led man to the moon and Mars. Oddly enough, the path also led to an awakening of the spirit that shook the foundations of established institutions. Not the least of these was that venerable institution known as public education.

> We stand today in the dawn of our second century and assess the field of future education. Surrounded by the greatest array of learning paraphernalia we have ever seen, and immersed in new knowledge, we must not lose sight of the human needs that the new dawn brings. We are at once the heirs of the past and the stewards of the future, and while we take pride in our inheritance, we can ill afford to bury our talents in the souls of satisfaction. We have in our hands means of change for

* Neil entered school in 1980, at the age of three, on a part-time basis.

8

human betterment that few people of the world enjoy. We must find a way to their application that will germinate the seeds of a more fruitful way of life, not only for the people of Ontario but for all Canadians; and hopefully the harvest will make its contribution to all mankind.

In such a climate were the seeds of change in Ontario education planted in the latter half of the twentieth century. In such a climate men found the determination and the desire to commit their efforts, not to the maintenance of an educational system to serve as the utilitarian handmaiden of the culture, but to the development of an atmosphere of learning that would nurture the sensitivity, the dignity, the awe, the commitment, and the uniqueness that are the rights of all men. Such men abandoned their traditional preoccupation with the past that had so long been their defence; the present they viewed with caution lest it lock them in. They looked instead to the future—the future of Neil Alexander Ellis; and they laid the way, not for themselves, but for him.

> Like the men who make the initial landing on the Moon, our children must be thoroughly prepared for a destination whose features no one knows at first hand. But this is not the first time that man has found himself in this position. The world presented as significant a challenge for the age of Columbus as it does for us half a millenium later. The achievements of the past are there to orient our youth; the vision, the speculation and the prediction for the future are there to challenge and excite their minds; it becomes a function of the school to provide that orientation and foster that excitement.

The public education of Neil Alexander Ellis really began four months before he was born. It was at this point that his mother, encouraged to realize her responsibility as a parent, used the facilities of the local school in order to study parent education. She was accepted and encouraged as a permanent member of the team destined to educate her youngster.

The school was more than a school. Gone were its time-honoured isolation as an academic cloister and its exclusive position as a factory for the manufacture of obedient adults. It stood as the cultural nerve centre of the community, and invited young and old to tap its resources and enjoy its excitement. As a community facility, it accurately reflected the needs, aspirations and interests of the people

9

whom it served. It was proof of the new awareness that democratic strength lies in diversity, not in uniformity, and it found its function at the local level rather than in remote authority. Nevertheless, since it was a place of learning, it was not only a local enterprise, but an investment in the future of the nation. Thus it was protected from local economic disparity by provincial and national funding with additional local option. Its trusteeship was regional, and an integral part of the regional government body; hence it was seen no longer as the annual cesspool for misspent money, but as a focal point of common public interest.

The same principle applied at the provincial level, where education was considered an integral part of all branches of government related to cultural welfare. In this way education not only found its rightful place among its related fields of health, welfare and rehabilitation; it also enjoyed the close co-ordination of those agencies so vital to its function. As a protection against bureaucratic and political complexity and insensitivity, an autonomous, non-political council representative of professional and lay interests served in an advisory capacity at the provincial level, reporting regularly to the public, and responsible to the Legislature. At the school level, a School Committee comprised of faculty and community members served as a reflection of local interest and commitment.

Public education for Neil was free of tuition costs throughout the spectrum formerly known as elementary, secondary and tertiary levels. It provided a continuous learning experience from the moment of initial entry until his entry into the tertiary level, individualized to the greatest possible degree, in keeping with his aptitudes, interests and abilities

Gone were the traditional trademarks of schooling that had so little to do with learning; grade placement, report card marks, formal examinations, annual promotion, failure, segregation, punishment, memorization of inert fact, regimentation, solemn purpose, and fear. In their place was found an atmosphere of humane understanding, warm, embracing, provocative, exciting, challenging, and completely committed to the nourishment of the spirit as well as the mind, to the fulfilment of life as well as of learning.

Gone, too, from the early levels of Neil's learning experience was the ancient parade of disciplines that had been the traditional hoops through which children were made to jump. Realizing the need for

10

synthesis in the development of attitudes and abilities, great care was taken to provide opportunities for the discovery of relevance in ideas and in things. To be sure, as the student proceeded toward maturity, his areas of study became more specific and specialized. But even then, the "wholistic" nature of life was not abandoned. Neil's desire to become an engineer was satisfied; but more important, so was his inclination to become a man.

It was not that the school had abandoned its academic role. Indeed, it was intensified—for those inclined. But the disciplines of the ages had taken on a new identity, alive, real and tantalizing to the student. Algebraic equations now beckoned Neil, not into the dead dust of the past, but into new possibilities for the future. Many new fields of study had appeared, some of them not even remotely related to the world of work. It was at last permissible to follow an interest that led nowhere except to maturity. Learning for its own sake had finally donned the cloak of respectability.

Neil entered school in 1980, at the age of three, on a part-time basis. His entry was based entirely upon his apparent needs and abilities as mutually accepted and determined by school and home. He entered his advanced level of education (university) thirteen years later. In the interim he experienced an educational program which had the following salient characteristics beyond those already noted:

*a school year based upon a tri-semester calendar, established by regional option.

*eye and dental care as an integral part of the educational service.

*a clinical approach to the identification and satisfaction of emotional, psychological and physical needs of each individual.

*a curricular program designed locally to meet the needs and interests of the school community.

*an atmosphere for learning that was more aesthetic than utilitarian, more general than specific.

*a flexibility of program that provided for maximum attention to the changing interests and abilities of the learners.

*maximum mobility to permit the realistic study of the environment.

*an emphasis upon learning experiences provided through discovery and research.

11

Of course, these conditions which Neil experienced were not created by legislation in 1980. Most, if not all of them, had been pleaded for long before his time. Indeed, not a few of them had already found their way into schools and systems of schools. But old ideas die hard, and complacency was always their protecter. Only when the people were struck with the awesome awareness of the huge price to be paid for means without ends did they see the need for revitalizing the process of living and of learning. Only then did they appreciate where the journey to Mars had brought them: to the stark realization that beyond the reach of man lies the beauty of the rose; that the search for truth and meaning was far from over. It had just begun. And so they dedicated their resources to the end that Neil Alexander Ellis, and others like him, would carry the search beyond the confines of the past and present into a future that knows no bounds.

The needs of the child are simply stated. Each and every one has the right to learn, to play, to laugh, to dream, to love, to dissent, to reach upward, and to be himself. Our children need to be made to feel that the world is waiting for their sunrise, and that their education heralds the rebirth of an "Age of Wonder". Then, surely, the children of tomorrow will be more flexible, more adventurous, more daring and courageous than we are, and better equipped to search for truth, each in his own way. Each will have learned, with Don Quixote, in *Man of La Mancha:*

> To dream the impossible dream,
> To fight the unbeatable foe,
> To bend with unbearable sorrow,
> To run where the brave dare not go.
> To right the unrightable wrong,
> To love, pure and chaste from afar,
> To try when one's arms are too weary,
> To reach the unreachable star.

The transition of the foregoing from hypothesis to reality is dependent upon a number of fundamental changes in educational theory and practice. Some are already in the process. Others are more remote, and perhaps a few are beyond our present reach. All are worthy of serious consideration by those bold enough to break new ground.

We are still caught up with the tribal custom of teaching the

12

young in the ways of their elders. We find it difficult, and even disturbing, to abandon the practice of distributing knowledge to be consumed as a commodity. As a productive society, we have become rather adept at measurement, control, organization, assembly, and the assessment of success by visible evidence. In the process, we are in danger of allowing the matter of material spill over into matters of the mind. Man does not go to a hall of learning merely to become a product of society. He goes to find a way, hopefully a better way. The role of the school is therefore not so much to reflect the culture as to lead it. It can only do this by offering itself as an arena where men of tomorrow come to wrestle with the possible and the unknown. In such an arena, teachers provide the challenge rather than the answers, the draught rather than the damper. More important, the public must embrace the school as the beacon pointing to the front rather than the rear.

We have in our inheritance a deeply rooted idea that the road to "salvation" is a tortuous one, one that the young, especially, must learn to tread with solemn purpose. Hence we strive to control the young rather than guide them and punish or abandon rather than embrace them. Children are not "waiting in the vestibule of the mansion of life". Childhood itself is one of the rooms. One has only to visit a school where the teachers embrace this idea to witness the dividends. But it requires patience, empathy, competence, and a mature awareness of life itself to make the belief a reality in the school. Perhaps too many of us are unconvinced.

We have a penchant for facilities in education. Ontario has some of the finest schools in the world, as far as facilities for learning go. But they don't go far enough on the road to educational excellence. Some day soon we shall be forced to face the obvious: learning is a matter of the mind and the spirit. It is most likely to occur when human resources are considered to be the prerequisite to successful school education. When we are convinced that teacher education— and teacher competence—are more than a matter of "training", and more important than buildings, we shall have gone a long way in the "Age of Wonder".

Assuming that education is an exercise of the State, one is likely to assume that it should be State-controlled. But the word "control" has an odious overtone when applied to learning. It is easy to justify the early central control of education in Ontario. It was the one assurance of provision, a guarantee of at least a minimum standard and although we have come a long way since Ryerson's day, we developed a habit along the way. It was the habit of rule and regu-

13

lation, of surveillance and authority. Hence we now have County Boards of Education, but face a new temptation of shifting control from one camp to another. It is interesting to note that the Department of Education has not shrunk in size, nor have County Boards been so far noted for their lack of hierarchy. Ways must be found by which we can place the action where it belongs—in the school community.

Education is a costly venture, far beyond the financial ability of local regions. But it is more than that. It is a cultural investment in which all Canadians have a stake. Surely this realization should lead us to find a way of financing education totally from provincial and federal sources without loss of local prerogative.

We speak often of the public lack of appreciation for education; yet we are less vociferous when we examine the reasons why. Education is conducted in a cloistered camp, and the lay citizen learned long ago to avoid confronting that which he was deemed incapable of understanding. How then can we now expect his magnanimous commitment to the expensive course of education—especially since his own remembrance is not likely to quicken his interest?

Nevertheless, the public and especially parents, have the inherent right and societal responsibility to participate actively in the design of education. Would a School Committee endanger the school principal, or a Provincial Advisory Council impede the Minister of Education? Surely the chance would be well worth taking.

Everyone agrees that teachers have an awesome responsibility —charged as they are with the task of "educating" the province and the nation—by law. One can only wonder at the length of time it takes us to put into practice what we say in theory: that the learning process is too complex a process to be dealt with superficially. When all is said and done about education, this much we know: that students are the lifeblood of our future, and teachers have their fingers on the pulse. To fail one is to abandon the other.

3

Begin at the Beginning: Preferential Opportunities for the Disadvantaged
Tim Reid

There is a conflict of opinion concerning the priorities in education in Canada and Ontario today. It is a conflict of opinion that is now hardened by the October, 1966 Federal-Provincial "entente" that adult manpower training and retraining is a federal government responsibility while education (defined as the imparting of knowledge through a standard curriculum during the period of childhood, adolescence and youth) is a provincial government responsibility. The federal government has reasserted its concern with national and regional manpower requirements and is giving this concern priority by backing it up with large expenditures. What has happened since 1965 is that the federal government has shifted upwards to an entirely new level in its manpower programs. Such an initiative was essential if Canada was serious about maintaining its place in the world as a highly productive economic system.

The provincial governments continue to state that one of the most important goals of their formal public education systems is the provision of full opportunities for the development of individual potential. Yet, since 1965 they have *not* shifted to a new level in their concern and in their financial support of such opportunities especially at the pre-high school level.

As a result, a new structure of *national* priorities in education and training has been established in Canada. It may also set the pattern for the 1970s in Canada and Ontario. First of all, adult training and re-training for the world-of-work has been given a much higher value relative to child and youth education for the development of the individual as an individual rather than as a factor of production. Secondly, adult training and re-training for the world-of-work has been given a new, higher value relative to adult education for the sake of continuing to learn, that is "as an end in itself and a contribution to how we live as civilized human beings". It is simply noted here that this latter shift in national priorities has taken place. The basic

15

concern in this essay is with the first shift in priorities.

Primary and pre-primary school education is the area in which a substantial upward shift in expenditures could have the greatest long-run individual, social, economic and political return.

On the one hand, there is the question of preparing individuals for the world-of-work and of maximizing their contribution to economic growth in this era of permanent scientific and technological revolution (popularly called "The Age of Automation"). For this goal, for *each* additional one million dollars invested today in pre-primary school education there could be a reduction by at least several million dollars in the expenditures that will be necessary to train and re-train many of today's four and five year olds fourteen years from now for the radically changed world-of-work of 1984. If, in other words, the approach to preparing individuals for the world-of-work had a deeper and longer-run perspective in decision-making than it has at present, Canada would have a much more rational and efficient allocation of funds today. On the other hand, there is the belief that it is good for an individual, however gifted, to be able to develop and use the gifts with which he was born. And related to this is the belief that social and economic barriers which stand between a child and the development of his inherited creative, intellectual, and physical gifts ought to be eliminated. For this goal, for *each* additional one million dollars spent today in pre-primary and primary school education there could be a reduction by several million dollars in the amount that will be spent on programs to counteract alienated teenagers ten years from now in 1980.

The conclusion about these two goals is that there is no valid dichotomy between training individuals to be productive and their education as unique human beings with unique gifts *at the pre-primary and primary school level.*

In Canada today a great deal of the intelligence, creativity, and other inherited abilities of a vast number of people is being wasted. At least one of every four non-farm Canadian families lives on an annual income of $4,000 or less and more than one of every two farm families live on $2,500 or less. At the very most 20 of every 100 children of such families in the age group 19 to 24 are attending a regular daytime school or university. Now if only 20 of every 100 of these children were born with the abili y to pursue such education, then the argument that there is a massive wastage of the talents of

Canadians would lose much of its validity. But this is not so. Since it is probable that more than 50 of every 100 young people 19 to 25 whose parents have annual incomes of $7,000 or more are still pursuing full-time school or university studies, then one-half of the young people whose parents have incomes of $4,000 or less can be judged as having been born with the capabilities of pursuing such education. (There may be more "born bright-but-poor" young people not involved in formal study than there are actually studying.) This "participation gap" is evidence of a massive wastage of manpower resources in Canada.

The federal government's Department of Labour noted in a case study in Ontario in the 1950s that "it is quite clear that children from 'middle class' and professional homes enjoy a higher 'survival rate' in the educational system than would be predicted from an examination of patterns according to which intelligence is distributed among students . . . . Such findings . . . merely underline the wastage that is occurring among the bright students who drop out of school not because of lack of intelligence or academic potential, but for economic, psychological and social reasons".

Indeed, the Bladen Report (*Financing Higher Education in Canada*) implies that for every two Canadians in universities today there is about one other young Canadian born with the same ability to do university work who is not attending a university.

The evidence noted above is based primarily on studies done in the 1950s and on the national census of 1961.. In 1965-66, the Canadian Union of Students did a large sample survey of Canadian undergraduate students which verified the conclusions of earlier studies that Canadian university students are "by and large not representative of the Canadian class structure but rather bear the characteristics of the middle and upper classes of Canadian society". For example, the study concluded that only 35.0 percent of Canadian university students were from "blue collar" or working-class families compared to 64.1 percent of employed Canadians who held jobs that could be so classified.

(Given the extent of this wastage, it is not at all surprising that, proportionately, there are more than twice as many young people in the United States pursuing higher education as there are in Canada.)

Now some people find nothing startling in these comparisons. They assert that children born into the lower social-economic strata

17

in Canada (for example, low-paid manual workers) are biologically inferior in their inherited abilities, particularly in their thinking powers, to children born to parents who are at the other end of the social-economic spectrum (for example, highly paid corporation directors). Theirs is a hereditary assumption which may have some validity in half a dozen isolated rural areas in Canada in which a great deal of family intermarriage has taken place over generations, but it is nonsense when applied to Ontario or to Canada as a whole. There is little evidence to support the assertion that the range and distribution of intelligence of a group of children born to parents who have not gone beyond Grade 8 and who bring home annual incomes of $4,000 or less is any different from the range and distribution of inherited capacity of a group of children born to parents with university education who bring home annual incomes of $7,000 or more. The number of children born with the capability for higher education is the same regardless of the social, educational, and economic background of their parents. This is the only possible premise to adopt in the formulation of public policy. It is unequivocally the operating principle of the United States War on Poverty as proposed by President Johnson in his message preceding the Economic Opportunity Act of 1964:

> The young man or woman who grows up without a decent education . . . in a hostile and squalid environment . . . that young man or woman is often trapped in a life of poverty. He does not have the skills demanded by a complex society. He does not know how to acquire those skills. He faces a mounting sense of despair which drains initiative and ambition and energy . . . . The war on poverty . . . is a struggle to give people a chance.

There are many reasons for the present wastage of human potential in Canada. The concern here is with the "poverty" environment only. It is now a platitude to say that it is the home environment which stimulates a child to develop the gifts with which he is born and stimulates his desire for learning and knowledge. There are tremendous differences between the home environment and attitudes of a poverty-handicapped home and a well-to-do home besides the definitional difference of annual incomes.

Thelma McCormack, a York University sociologist, comments:

> The poverty syndrome is produced not by economic depriva-

tion but by a pattern of social relations symbolized and maintained by income differences. Being poor means being powerless, being treated in a variety of contexts throughout one's life . . . . The Old Left called these people the 'lumpenproletariat' to suggest that they were not just poorer than most but outcasts too. The probability is high that their children will be outcasts too. Everything conspires against them. With few exceptions their fate is sealed before they ever walk across the threshold of schools which would have failed them in any event.

One essential aspect of the "poverty syndrome" is that "poverty homes" produce too many children without adequate words at the age of four and five. Such children have not had the opportunity or the encouragement to pick up the basic skills of communication and understanding of language that are largely a prerequisite for success in senior kindergarten and Grade 1.

All later learning will be influenced by this lack of basic learning . . . having names for things is essential in the learning process! The average child from such a background will have difficulty and constant frustration from the demand of a typical primary school program. He cannot cope with the change and with teacher expectations about what he should achieve, and he is baffled and feels inadequate. No wonder the desire grows to escape from the virtual imprisonment which school comes to represent as he experiences failure year after year. Instead of eight or ten years of primary school curing the basic handicap of such a child, he has either left school for good or if he lasts through secondary school, is probably reading, and able to communicate, at a level approximately three and one half years below the expected grade average. Since he literally cannot read the secondary school arts and sciences text books of Grade 9 it is probable that he will shift into the stream, labelled in Ontario as "science, technology and trades", "business and commerce", and "occupational". In too many cases, the choice is simply to get out of the tough reading courses of the university-geared arts and science programs. A great many gifted children from poverty homes end up in courses below the level of their actual intelligence because they *appear* to lack the ability. Most do not get into the academic stream leading to university and many other kinds of post secondary school education.

Most provincial departments of education in Canada have recently re-organized the secondary school curriculum. In Ontario the re vision instituted in the early 1960s has resulted in an extraordinary perversion of intent. Although it was clearly not planned as such, it has turned out to be "class" legislation in the sense that it encouraged children from lower-income homes to stay out of the five year stream leading to a university and reserved places in that stream for the sons and daughters of the well-to-do. This happened because the reorganization of the secondary school curriculum was not backed up by a barrage of other educational measures designed for the very young, disadvantaged, and poor children and their parents. The reorganization accentuated rather than diminished the enormous gap between those who can and do read and communicate intelligently—between those who can and do communicate in the language of the school—and those to whom the printed word and the standard techniques of communication in the school setting mean very, very little.

In the 1960s several provincial departments of education also expanded non-university institutions of higher education, particularly the junior college. Excellent examples of these are the community colleges established in British Columbia and Alberta. A somewhat different trend has been taking place in Ontario. Ontario established Colleges of Applied Arts and Technology (CAATs) which are merely a logical extension of the secondary school organization plan. The CAATS in Ontario are, unless substantial policy changes are made in the earlier 1970s, in effect sealing the fate of the average culturally disadvantaged pupil who survives four years of secondary school in a watered-down stream, particularly in the stream labelled "4 years arts and science". The principle of "separate but equal education" has now been institutionalized in post secondary school education in Ontario. Instead of the colour of one's skin being the distinguishing characteristic, poor or well-to-do family background have become, in general, the *de facto* entrance labels. The two plans together, in Ontario, have progressively closed the door to re-entry to the top level of academic education after Grade 8 to those many teenagers who are placed at an absolute and at a competitive disadvantage because of the accident of birth.

The priority in education today in Ontario must be at the primary and pre-primary school level. Many educators and experts on learning accept the validity of the following statement by A.R. Jensen.

20

Our present knowledge of the development of learning abilities indicates that the pre-school years are the most important years of learning in the child's life. A tremendous amount of learning takes place during these years; and this learning is the foundation for all further learning.

A further statement by Jerome Bruner supports this concept.

It is not surprising in the light of this that early opportunities for development have loomed so large in our recent understanding of human mental growth. The importance of early experience is only dimly sensed to-day. The evidence from animal studies indicates that *virtually irreversible deficits can be produced in mammals by depriving them of opportunities that challenge their nascent capacities.*

It is on the basis of this premise that the advocates of pre-primary school education for children born into the "poverty syndrome" largely rest their case. For example, the multifarious "Head Start" program in the United States rests on the assumption that an organized program of enrichment preceding kindergarten or first grade schooling will have an important positive effect on the educational and social development of children living in conditions of poverty".

In Canada the number of "five year olds" increased by 50 percent between 1951 and 1964 (from 301,000 to 454,000). The number of five year olds *in school* is estimated to have increased over the period by almost 200 percent (from 92,000 to 271,000). This means that the percentages of 5 year olds in school almost doubled (from 31 percent in 1951 to 60 percent in 1964). These results are praiseworthy.

A closer look, however, reveals some interesting facts:

1. The Dominion Bureau of Statistics states that in 1964, 19 percent of all the five year olds in British Columbia attended public and private elementary schools compared to 96 percent in Nova Scotia.
2. In the Ontario Public School system in 1964 only 3 of every 100 pupils in rural townships were in kindergarten compared to over 12 of every 100 pupils in cities.
3. In the City of Toronto which has one of the most extensive systems of junior kindergarten classes in Canada, the following statement was a major conclusion of a study (1965) by the Research Division of the Board of Education:

Junior kindergarten is most available in areas characterized by low socio-economic and educational levels of the parents

21

> . . . children from the lower socio-economic strata might
> benefit by the extra year . . . . *But these are not the children
> who are sent to junior kindergarten.*

4. In Ontario the number of five year olds in kindergarten in the
Public School system increased by 40 percent between 1956 and
1961; the increase in the Roman Catholic Separate Schools was
107 percent. Looked at from a different index, an index of
"kindergarten enrolment to total enrolment", the increase was
10 percent in the Public Schools between 1956 and 1964 and 98
percent in the Roman Catholic Separate Schools. (It should be
noted that in 1964, 9.5 percent of the pupils in Public School were
in kindergarten and 8.6 percent of the pupils in Roman Catholic
Schools were in kindergarten.)

5. In Ontario there are about 160,000 five year olds. Ten years from
now there may well be 187,000: an increase of 27,000 (17 percent).

Various interpretations can be given to these facts. One set of
tentative conclusions could be the following. There are vast provincial opportunity gaps in Canada for five year olds to attend school.
Within each province (Nova Scotia excepted) there are vast regional
opportunity gaps for five year olds to attend school. Within areas in
which junior Public School kindergartens for four and five year olds
(Toronto for example) are widely available, the children of the lower
socio-economic strata are vastly under-represented. In one province
(Ontario) the Roman Catholic Separate Schools made a much greater
relative thrust at the pre-Grade 1 level over the last decade than did
the Public School sector. Over the next decade there could well be a
normal 17 percent increase in the number of five year olds in Canada.
(There could, of course, be a dramatic downward shift in the Canadian birth rate).

The children who will be in their early twenties in 1985 are
already born. The vast majority of the 30 percent of five year olds
who are *not* attending school are from poverty and low income
families — children who were born behind the eight ball of disadvantage, children who need *preferential* pre-primary school education if
they are to have a meaningful chance to develop the abilities with
which they were born and have an equal chance in competition in
school against the children from more affluent and advantaged homes.
In the world of 1985 it is doubtful that very many of these children

will feel like worthwhile citizens and independent members of society; their process of alienation started the day they were born and little is being done before they are six years old to help them lift themselves up. Virtually *nothing* is being done for them when they are four years old, an age which some learning experts state is much, much more potentially productive than five years old.

It is difficult to predict what the effects of the new technology will be on Canadian society, particularly in education and the world-of-work. Nevertheless, the following speculative view represents a state of affairs that might *possibly* come about.

The evidence of an extremely wide gap between the level of formal education reached by the children of the relatively well-to-do and the level reached by the children of the poor has been noted above, as has been other evidence indicating the sheer magnitude of the under-representation of children from low income homes in Canada's educational institutions, particularly in post secondary school institutions. Regardless of the reasons why children born into low income homes do not occupy anything near their share of places now available in the final years of high school and beyond, the clear fact is that they do not. It can be argued that what the new technology is beginning to do is to freeze those conditions in our society which tend to perpetuate the sons and daughters of the poor in the cycle of poverty and to perpetuate the sons and daughters of the middle class and wealthy in the cycle of middle class and wealth. The basic reason for this ossification could be that, for the first time in the history of man, education is placed squarely between man and the work which is his acceptable means of livelihood. Thus, the children of the poor tend to be dropouts from elementary and secondary school education. These under-educated members of the labour force are increasingly becoming the unemployed. The unemployed are the poor. The children of the poor are the school dropouts and so on. Even if the average child from a low income home survives to secondary school, he ends up in an academically watered-down technical, commercial, or liberal arts stream for two to four years to prepare for a low grade and low income job, which—particularly if he happens to be born quite bright—is usually personally unrewarding.

In the industrial economy in the pre-1960s he probably managed to get a steady job and considered himself fortunate to have achieved the same low income category as his parents. Today, and in the

23

future world of automation, however, the likelihood of the average person with such an educational background securing a steady job. will be much less. Instead he will join the ranks of the occasional labourer and eventually take his place as a welfare recipient, possibly before he is twenty-five. If his children have only the opportunities he had to make his way in life, then the saying "If they're poor now, they will never be anything else" will tell the story from one generation to the next.

The other cycle is just the reverse. The children of the relatively well-to-do stay in school, and some of the less able enter and scrape through a university. The highly educated are the employed who receive good middle class salaries. The children of the middle class stay in school. The average child from the middle income home will get into the academic stream in secondary school which has an "open door" to universities. He will end up with a good job and a good salary to enable him to hand on a middle class life to his children. The shift from the industrial age to the age of automation will certainly affect his life but it will not cut his job and income out from under his feet.

Unless, therefore, the link between dropouts from education and young people from low income homes is *broken* before the full impact of the new technology makes itself felt in the world-of-work, automation could virtually eliminate social mobility from one generation to the next. The poor and their children will not only be alienated from education but will, as a direct consequence, be alienated from participation in the productive process, and fail to receive any income from such participation. This could mean increasing alienation of such individuals from society.

This speculative view of the "new technology and opportunity" should be considered. It could happen. However, if the right policies are taken today it need not happen and the possibility need not exist.

In some of the better-financed and socially concerned school board districts in Canada, the need, and hardheaded economic returns, have been identified and action taken. The Board of Education of the City of Toronto has been mentioned already as having an outstanding example of a school board which is trying to fight its war on poverty without a moral or financial commitment from other levels of government. Another example is the ENOC pro-

24

gram in Hamilton, Ontario. ENOC stands for "Educational Needs of the Older City". The ENOC program is designed to uplift many of the children in the older and poorer areas of the city who are greatly handicapped by circumstances: unemployed fathers, broken homes, inferior housing conditions, large families, lack of parental concern and interest. (Only half of the parents from such areas attended the school "open house" compared to an almost complete attendance of parents at a school in a middle income area in the city). The ENOC program includes a kindergarten for four year olds with emphasis on remedial reading, teacher visits to the home of each child, medical examinations for each child, and in some cases dental examinations ("children whose teeth hurt can't study"), and trips and excursions in order to broaden the experience of the children and to increase their vocabulary. Surely, if such opportunities are given to disadvantaged children in Hamilton, they should also be offered to similarly disadvantaged children throughout Ontario and Canada. They would have opportunities not only to develop individual potentials but to become trained and educated to make their way in life in the world-of-work of the age of automation; it is manpower training at the beginning.

We must recognize that adult manpower training for jobs in 1985 has a basic relationship with, and is highly dependent on, what happens in the way of training and education at the pre-primary school level today. What is then needed is a federal ministry of manpower and anti-poverty which would have as one of its cornerstones a program of pre-primary school *training* for disadvantaged children, combined with a fundamental shift in priorities in education by the Ontario Government. A real combined "war on poverty" and "manpower training program" would have many other objectives, but the pre-primary school front would be the major one and would have the greatest long-run economic, personal, and social benefits.

The first public-policy principle that must be accepted in Canada and Ontario is that of universal accessibility to education. The first program to achieve genuine accessibility to education is one that makes it possible for children born into low income homes to have as good a set of initial communication skills, by at least the age of five, as children of equal inherited ability from homes of the well-to-do. Our kindergartens are certainly not even attempting to do this. Many children from low income homes have been born into a poverty syndrome and they need preferential treatment in education, not simply equal treatment. This is not happening, particularly in our rural areas. Furthermore, our nursery schools have children who are mainly from well-to-do homes where the exact opposite ought to be true. Quite simply, without universal opportunity *before* kindergarten and Grade 1, it is impossible to have universal accessibility to education that will enable a child to develop the gifts with which he was born. The hard fact which has at least been recognized in the United States but not in Canada and Ontario is that five years old is too late for the underprivileged child to begin schooling.

4

Ontario Universities in a New Society
John B. MacDonald

Prophecy is an uncertain trade and can be hazardous. It has been related to witchcraft, tea-cup readers, fortune tellers and "con" artists. When practiced as a science, or a legitimate business, it is hardly less subject to error, as any observer of the stock market or even the fortunes of political parties will tell you. The kindest thing that can be said about it is that forecasting is an inexact science. Nevertheless, I would like to peer into the future of university education in Ontario, for only in this way can we organize our affairs and order our priorities.

I must define my assumptions before I try to peer into a glass darkly. My first assumption is that one can extrapolate from the recent past to project what will happen in the near future. Here I am talking specifically about the last few years and the next ten years: What has happened in higher education? What will happen?

My second assumption is that a good indicator of the future is the voice of youth, for the future belongs to youth. It will be their values and their dreams for which man will strive. This is not to say that all of their proposals for solutions will prevail. As with past generations, experience will temper their impatience and their stridency; but those fundamental goals for which they speak will remain and will colour their attitudes and their choices in the years ahead.

Youth today is demanding a society that places a premium on human values, and a discount on material goals. The key to understanding youth may be in a statement by Nobel laureate, George Wald. "The present generation of students is the first in history to be unsure it has a future."* Extinction through nuclear holocaust is an ever-present threat. At the same time communication and transportation technology have created the global village where each can see the sights and hear the sounds of man's inhumanity, his greed,

* Wald, G., *New Yorker,* Mar. 22, 1969.

27

his aggressiveness and his ruthless desecration of his environment. Youth today rejects the hypocrisy of societies that talk peace while arming to the teeth. They know that with present trends, by the year 2000 overcrowding will have become extreme. Yet they see no policies to control population. They see poverty and know that while politicians use noble words to express our concern, the rich nations get richer and the poor get poorer. Youth sees man flying to the moon and yet unable to stem the pollution of air and water, so serious that men like Barry Commoner have stated that "this planet is approaching a crisis which may destroy its suitability as a place for human society" *

Youth sees society "rife with myopic and self-righteous belief in a 'progress' that is defined almost wholly in materialistic and power-centered terms of immediate gain" **

Though rejecting what it sees, youth has reacted often in ways which are far from constructive. The nihilistic revolutionaries see only as far as the destruction of society's institutions − initially the university as a symbol of society and because it is easily accessible and highly vulnerable. Larger numbers have adopted an existentialist view of life. Seeing no certain future for themselves or their children, they concern themselves with the present and demand instant solutions to complex problems. Still others vent their frustrations and their feelings of helplessness in symbolic demonstrations against the war in Vietnam, against racial discrimination, against ghetto landlords, against the military-industrial complex. They demonstrate in ways that show more concern for form and the strengthening of ties with their generation than with rational analysis and orderly solution to problems.

Let none of these shortcomings mislead you. Youth is the establishment of tomorrow and I predict and indeed pray that their clear identification of many of the real issues confronting mankind will be coupled with hard-headed and vigorous attack on the problems. If their deep sense of human values survives, they can be the great hope of the future.

* Commoner, B., a statement made at Annual Meeting, American Associations for the Advancement of Science, December, 1967.

** Shoben, J., from Minneman, C.E. (Ed.), *Students, Religion and the Contemporary University,* Eastern Michigan University Press, 1969.

How do these views relate to the future of higher education in Ontario? What qualitative changes are demanded? What are the quantitative problems? How should our great university enterprise be related to the public interest?

Along with the emergence of new values which will affect every businessman, every member of the professions and every politician, certain other conditions are likely to prevail.

1) Technology will continue to advance, hopefully harnessed to humane priorities. This will place increased demands on higher education to provide an increasing variety of specialists to fill society's needs.

2) Technology and automation will increase productivity and shorten the average work week.

3) An increase in leisure time coupled with increased demand for retraining as jobs become obsolete and new jobs arise will involve more and more adults of all ages in continuing higher education.

4) The demands and needs of adults of all ages will be for a broadening of their intellectual opportunity to provide not just specialist qualification but a better understanding of the world in which they live and a deeper appreciation of the human condition.

This change is already upon us as changing values and changing attitudes prompt youth to call for more relevance in education. This demand is usually misunderstood or misinterpreted. I believe it represents dissatisfaction with education that produces only specialists and lacks the breadth and majesty to confront the great issues which cannot be solved by the specialist alone. I believe it represents a call for more attention to moral issues and human concerns, to supplement agnostic expertise. I believe it signifies not a rejection of specialism but a conviction that education must transcend specialism.

Highly pertinent to this point of view is a quotation from Joseph Shoben:*

It can be cogently argued that higher education is shockingly poor—almost deliberately inattentive to the difficulties of personal development that beset undergraduates, much too frequently far removed from the problems that buffet students

* Shoben, J., from Minneman, C.E. (Ed.), *Students, Religion and the Contemporary University,* Eastern Michigan University Press, 1969.

outside the college's boundaries, overly preoccupied with the strategies of an increasingly specialized and professionalized scholarship while quite unimaginative with respect to the processes of learning and teaching, and inclined to present only the model of the don as an image of adult life against which students can react in defining their own identity and their own style. Moreover, for many thoughtful and concerned critics of the university scene, the reformist ideas of students often seem more constructive and more insightful than do the occasional tinkerings of faculty with instructional curricular affairs. With respect to grading policies, curricular structures, the relationship of instructional devices to the improvement of learning, and the ways in which habits of reflection can be more tightly bound to an enlarging reservoir of experience, the student voice has typically been informed, reasoned and questing.

These considerations of the quality of university education will have the effect of adding significantly to the quantitative demands in the years ahead. Those demands by mere extrapolation will be very large. I therefore have no hesitation in saying that the demands which our society in Ontario will place on higher education will be such that this enterprise will come to represent a greater and greater share of our total human, physical and financial resources.

University enrolment in Ontario doubled in the 5 years between 1964 and 1969 to a figure of 95,000. Operating grants grew from $57 million to $215 million. Capital grants grew from $64 million in 1964 to $100 million in 1969. Approved capital expenditures between July 1964 and December 1967 amounted to $377 million. Concurrently with this staggering rate of growth we have witnessed the establishment of 8 new universities and 10 new campuses in the province. Impressive as are these figures they tell only part of the story. The colleges of applied arts and technology were established only in 1965. Twenty colleges have been launched with a current enrolment of 22,000 day students and 28,000 extension students. They offer usually from 30 to 50 different programs of about 1 to 3 years' duration and in spite of their extraordinary growth have been unable to keep up with the demand.

Post-secondary education in Ontario, as in most jurisdictions in the western world, has experienced unprecedented growth. The precedent is about to be repeated. University enrolments are expected to double again by 1976. By extrapolation they will reach at least -

240,000 by 1981. That means that Ontario is faced with providing in 1981 for nearly 2½ times as many university students as will be enrolled in 1969-70. Another way of looking at it is to say that we must in the next 10 years provide more university buildings and more student places than we have built in this century or, for that matter, since Confederation.

Staggering as this growth appears, I predict that these extrapolations represent a substantial underestimate of what we face and what we will accomplish. The predicted enrolment in universities for 1981 equals about 21 percent of the age group 18-24. Ten years ago only 5.3 percent of the 18-24 year olds were enrolled. The participation rate will, I predict, increase faster than extrapolation suggests because of increased interest in and opportunity for general education, increased demand for retraining in the professions and highly skilled fields, and a growing demand for intellectual pursuits in the adult population.

As a measure of the task ahead let us make a conservative estimate of the cost of operating the universities in 1981. Present operating costs are $250 million (including tuition fees). Assume a 6 percent annual escalation in cost (and it is difficult to see how it could be kept that low). Assume what I believe to be a conservative estimate of enrolment in 1981: namely 240,000 students. (The Ontario Institute for Studies in Education has published projections running as high as 271,000 students.) Assuming, then, these conservative forecasts, the direct operating costs of Ontario universities will be about one billion dollars in 1981.

Is meeting that projection an impossibility? I think not. University education will hold a high priority for the people of Ontario. Moreover, it is a documented fact that there is an intimate relationship between investment in higher education and economic productivity both for nations and individuals. Our investment in higher education measured by relative enrolments has been less than in the United States of America and it will be 8 years before we catch up to the present level of enrolment in the U.S. I know of no concern in the U.S. that investment in higher education in that country is reaching a point of diminishing returns. Still, the financial demands on Ontario for university education up to 1981, proportionately, will far outstrip the growth of the gross provincial product. This can only mean that the commitment to university education must rise disproportionately

31

if the predicted demand is to be met. Since I believe the public in our province will place a high priority on higher education, I believe the government in power over these years will need to find ways to meet the demand.

I turn now to the relationship between universities and government in the years ahead.

Ontario has 14 self-governing universities. That in my judgment is a fortunate circumstance. Universities are likely to perform imaginatively and achieve excellence only if they can define their own goals and organize their own programs in such a way as to achieve those goals. Whatever system of control and coordination develops in this province, its purpose should be to encourage the development of the greatest possible strength in the individual universities of the system. I subscribe to the viewpoint expressed by John Dale Russell writing about higher education in Michigan: "Strength in an institution is closely associated with autonomy in the making of essential decisions affecting the institution's operations. It is virtually impossible to build a strong institution of higher education unless it is given the maximum of self determination in its operations."* That view obviously is not shared by everyone. Those who support the concept of a University of Ontario place a high premium on coordination, economy, efficiency in the use of dollars and uniformity of standards. Some coordination is necessary and unnecessary duplication must be avoided. Uniformity, on the other hand, is not a desirable goal when it comes to higher education. To quote myself, or as Adlai Stevenson once said, "to coin my own phrase", I refer to comments which I made in British Columbia in 1962: "There is a fallacy in choosing a unified system. In seeking to guarantee minimum standards, the system, in fact, places a ceiling on standards. No institution can be better than the next. Credits are freely transferable from one institution to another — a grand design dedicated perforce to mediocrity. Whatever this is, it is not education at its best. No institution and no one system has the answer to what is best in education. Free enterprise here, as much or more than elsewhere in our society, is the essential key to progress. The proposition was expressed eloquently by Felix Schelling: 'True education makes for inequality,

* Russel, J.D., *The Final Report of the Survey of Higher Education in Michigan*, 1958.

32

the inequality of individuality, the inequality of success; the glorious inequality of talent, of genius. For inequality, not mediocrity — individual superiority, not standardization — is the measure of progress in the world'."*

To deal with the 14 universities in Ontario, the government has taken 2 important steps. In 1964 it established a Department of University Affairs, the first of its kind in Canada. The Department has for its Minister the same individual who serves as Minister of Education. It has, however, its own Deputy Minister and its own research staff. In addition to the Department of University Affairs, the government established in 1964 a Committee on University Affairs "to study matters concerning the establishment, development, operation, expansion and financing of Universities in Ontario, and to make recommendations thereon to the Minister of University Affairs for the information and advice of government". The Committee has 11 members, including a full-time Chairman and 4 members drawn from the universities. I think it fair to say that when the Committee on University Affairs was established, it was envisioned as an instrument interposed between the universities and government, interpreting for each the viewpoint of the other. In practice, the Committee on University Affairs has come to be prejudiced towards the government's side. This comment is not made as a criticism but rather as a statement of inevitability resulting from the pull of conflicting forces. On the one hand the government is confronted with a multiplicity of demand from many sources which it must adjust and balance. On the other hand, the universities must seek for their purposes the funds which they feel necessary to perform their functions at a high level of competence in an international academic world which is vigorously competitive. It is not surprising, therefore, that the government needs the advice of the Committee on University Affairs to permit it to judge how far it should go towards meeting the legitimate aspirations of the universities.

The universities, for their part, have their own instrument for helping them to coordinate their efforts and for allowing them to speak with a collective voice to the Committee on University Affairs and to government. This instrument is the Committee of Presidents

* Macdonald, J.B., *Higher Education in British Columbia and a Plan for the Future*, University of British Columbia, 1962.

of Universities of Ontario, which was established more or less formally in 1962 but which did not adopt a constitution until 1968.

The most important device used by the government, the Committee on University Affairs, and the universities for ensuring equitable treatment, accountability and autonomy, is formula financing. Operating grants are distributed to the universities on the basis of a certain number of dollars for each student enrolled. Different weights are applied to students in different programs depending in a very rough way on the costs of particular programs. The weights vary from 1 to 6. A dollar value is applied each year to a unit value of 1 and from this the income for each university can be computed. The system has important advantages and has, on the whole, been well received by the universities, and, I believe, is considered by government to be sound. In the first place it provides for equitable distribution of funds to each university. Also, it preserves the autonomy of institutions because once they receive the income generated by their enrolment, they are free to establish their own priorities and expend the funds as they see fit. The system also acts as an incentive for efficiency because, since each university is treated in exactly the same way, the university which manages its funds in the ablest way will achieve the most distinguished results. The formula provides automatically for enrolment increases. Finally, government can forecast with reasonable accuracy the magnitude of the support which it will find necessary to provide.

The formula can have one significant disadvantage. It was devised for the purpose of generating income for the universities and it was recognized from the beginning that it reflected costs in only a very general and rough way. Nevertheless, there has been a certain tendency for some administrators to feel that the formula should be allocated in the places that it is generated. That is, if a particular faculty generates a certain sum of money because of its enrolment, its administration may feel that the university should allocate that sum to the faculty. Such practice obviously would defeat the purpose of giving to each university autonomy in the use of its own funds.

As the system has grown and increased in complexity, the universities themselves and also the Committee on University Affairs have seen opportunities for coordination and cooperation. The Committee of Presidents, through its affiliates and its various committees, has attempted to exploit these opportunities. For example, progress has

34

been made toward the establishment of a provincial bibliographic centre sponsored by all 14 universities. A sum of money has been set aside to investigate opportunities for computer coordination and to explore the possibility and practicality of relying on a major computer facility to serve the whole system. Machinery has been established to review graduate programs in the province and to pass qualitative judgment on proposed new programs. A committee is studying ways of rationalizing further graduate development. Other committees are examining the impact and implications of the value of the basic income unit used in the operating grant formula. Yet another committee is examining, along with the Committee on University Affairs and a consulting firm, various ways of developing a capital formula.

All of these functions, until recently, have been carried out with no full-time research staff available to the Committee of Presidents. Moreover, the organization has been essentially representative of the administration of the universities, although there has been participation on the Committee of Presidents by academic colleagues. The agenda has grown as cooperative efforts have increased in numbers, and the presidents have found it increasingly difficult to give proper attention to the wide variety of issues which come before their Committee.

During the past year, serious attention has been given to extensive revision of the structure of the Committee of Presidents. A proposal for a new agency called the Council of Universities of Ontario to replace the present Committee of Presidents is now before the universities for their consideration. The basic purpose of the new Council would be threefold. First, to provide a collective voice for the universities which is both acceptable and functional. Second, to retain for each university the maximum independence consistent with achieving a level of province-wide coordination and cooperation necessary to ensure wise use of public funds. Third, to provide the universities with a research staff on a full-time basis capable of conducting the necessary analyses and studies and accumulating the necessary data to facilitate the adoption of wise collective policy, and to make sound recommendations to the government through the Committee on University Affairs.

In the proposal now under consideration, the Council would consist of the president of each university plus a colleague elected by the

35

senate of each university. The Council would serve as the senior deliberative body for the 14 universities. Reporting to the Council would be a series of program committees representing large groupings of the universities' activities, such as arts and science, health sciences, graduate studies. The Council and the program committees are to be served by a research staff responsible for operating a provincial data bank and conducting the analyses needed by the various groups.

The Council would deal with a wide variety of interests common to all the universities. For example, the Council through its research staff, would conduct studies aimed at estimating the necessary value of the basic income unit in the operating grant in order to make recommendation to the Committee on University Affairs. Similarly, it would make recommendations on the proposed capital formula. It would consider from time to time the need for changes in the structure of both the operating grants formula and a capital grants formula. While the universities cannot be responsible for manpower planning for the province as a whole, they need to cooperate with agencies of government in projecting manpower needs. The Council would seek a rationalized approach to program development in order to prevent unhealthy duplication of teaching and research facilities in the province. The Council would engage in cooperative enterprises to serve all the universities — for example, the proposed Ontario Bibliographic Centre and cooperative efforts in the field of computer services.

A crucial question is the power to be vested in the Council. Can 14 universities, acting voluntarily, delegate sufficient power to a central Council to permit decisions and policies to represent anything less than the least common denominator? That question remains unanswered. Certain conclusions will require the support of all 14 universities if the Council is to be effective. An example would be the value of the basic income unit as recommended to the Committee on University Affairs. Other conclusions might require voluntary restraint on the part of all 14 universities. An example could be an agreement on limits for enrolment of foreign graduate students. Still other conclusions will require the voluntary participation of all the universities. An example is the establishment of an Ontario Bibliographic Centre. Finally, some decisions can be made only by government and the best the universities could achieve would be overall agreement on a recommendation. An example would be agreement on a recommendation for the location of a new health sciences centre. In such a case competing universities would find it difficult, if not impossible, to share in the collective judgment. Perhaps the Council itself might find it impossible to reach a consensus. At the least, the Council, through its research staff, could provide background analyses of population trends, availability of hospitals, other health facilities, and professional personnel, all of which would bear on a decision which in the last analysis must be made by government.

The question can be asked in another way. Is the Council not just another name for the University of Ontario? The answer to this question is emphatically "no". State universities with many campuses are common in the United States and in general they share a number of characteristics which are not contemplated in the Council of Universities. Budget control is centralized so that funds are not distributed according to formula but according to the planning of some central authority. Capital programs likewise are centralized. The development of new programs is determined centrally, even to the point where new programs may be imposed on a campus contrary to its wishes. A centralized university authority is likely to exercise centralized control over appointments for the whole system. The campuses of the University of California fought vigorously against such control but in the spring of 1969 control was returned to the Board of Regents. Admissions policy and selection of students is likely to be subject to centralized control. All of these features are contrary to the spirit of the proposed Council of Universities.

It must be admitted that the University of Ontario is a viable alternative to the proposal for a Council of Universities and the argument in favour of a University of Ontario is a plausible one. Centralized, bureaucratic allocation of resources to each university on the basis of program budgeting may give the best insurance of the maximum efficiency in expenditure of educational dollars, but efficiency is not the ultimate goal. The real objective is a superb educational system. If there is to be quality, creativity and imagination, then freedom to experiment and innovate must be delegated widely. A system which gives each university a free hand in the use of resources allocated equitably is surely the best guarantee of excellence. Any loss in efficiency will be a small price to pay.

I have no doubts about the need for a centralized research organization. I have no doubts about the soundness of the proposed structure for the universities' collectivity, though details will vary and opportunities for improvement will become evident. Accepting that we are making a beginning, we have a good chance of demonstrating that 14 independent universities can work together in the public interest and provide an educational system of high quality. What we are doing is unique. If we are successful, we will not only serve our province well but we will offer a new and better model for others to emulate.

5

Social Policy for Ontario
Leonard Shifrin

The subject of this discussion is social policy. The idea of looking at an integrated totality called social policy, rather than at its individual components, is not of very long standing, even as an idea. As a functional principle, only the most preliminary and tentative steps have been taken anywhere. And the anywheres are very few and far between.

Social policy involves health, welfare, education, manpower and housing — to name just a few of its well-defined components. But social policy is also much more than the sum of its parts. To talk of the package instead of the parts is to start with a wholly different vantage. If we are talking social policy, then we are talking human development, a vastly different thing than the mere sum of health, welfare, manpower and such.

Human development means addressing ourselves to things far more basic than the tinkering with policies in traditional categories. Our starting point is the goal of individual self-fulfillment and a self-concept in relation to the social order in which the individual feels himself a part of the order, capable of affecting it and thus responsible in part for it.

It has long been contended that the degree of social mobility in a society is the measure of its success as a free, open and opportunist order. By this measure, the United States with more than 40 percent of its young people reaching post-secondary school level, is the most successful society anywhere and should therefore be the most tranquil. In fact, of course, it is undergoing the most convulsive of upheavals for the very reason that the social mobility measure is fallacious.

Inherent in equating social mobility with individual freedom and opportunity is the view of the social superstructure as a static pyramid with people moving up and down the ladders, settling into the various niches at the various levels. The structure is static, only the players move about.

It is this acceptance of the pyramid as the given that is today being challenged. Social change is radically different from social mobility. Social change involves, at a minimum, the restructuring of the pyramid and, some would contend, the elimination of pyramids altogether.

The view that what must change is the power structure itself and not just the mobility within it is what has led to the radicals' contention that liberalism is dead. Liberalism, they argue, cannot go beyond the opening of existing doors. Changes in the pattern of social organization and distribution of social power can only be achieved through the use of tactics incompatible with the sophisticated civility of liberalism.

This is the question which divides the liberals from the radicals. Can institutionalized patterns, even of thought, be transformed without the need of a cataclysmic event to shake the structure to its foundations?

I was presented with an interesting illustration of this question the other day by an American theoretician in the field of alienation. He pointed out that, asked to draw a simple organization chart reflective of administrative structures in general, people will invariably draw something like this.

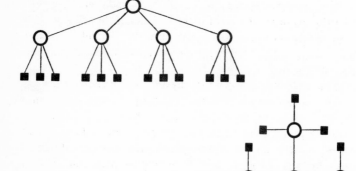

They would never think to draw this.

But if we look at the two, they are actually the same. Functionally they are identical. But psychologically they are worlds apart.

Instinctively we relate to the pyramid. Someone is on top and someone on the bottom. From the broad base to the narrow apex, layer is piled neatly on layer. The pecking order is neatly defined. The molecular structure, on the other hand, frightens us. There is a sensation that nothing is holding the molecules down; that the structure could disintegrate into chaos at any moment.

His point was, with identical lines of authority, power differences were the same in both cases. What had been changed were status differences. Without a vertical stratification, status differences had been reduced. Being toward the periphery of a circle did not carry the same psychological implications that being at the bottom of a pyramid did. Being at the center of a circle seemed far less awesome than standing at the pinnacle of a pyramid.

He argued that while efficient *administrative* organization required power differences, *social* organization did not. The power differences in social organization flowed from the unnecessary status differences we had built into all of our administrative structures.

Inherent in the pyramid is authoritarianism and it is the absence of this in the molecular circle that makes us uncomfortable with it. I should make clear that authoritarianism does not necessarily involve ill will. In fact, the authoritarianism which permeates our society is distinctly benevolent. It is the well-meaning benevolent authoritarianism of the parent toward the child.

What we are seeing today, on a wide variety of fronts, is the rejection of that paternalism which was the proud product of our liberal hour. A society in which no one cared for the forgotten man was transformed by us liberals because we cared. We built the welfare state because we cared. We provided for compulsory schooling because we cared. We built a hodgepodge of benevolent structures because *we* cared about *them*. And *we* ran these for *them*. Because *we* knew what was best for *them*.

Part of the reason why that system is under attack relates simply to the fact that we never funded it adequately to do the job we said it was designed to do. But there is a far more basic reason, which would be there even if this had not been the case.

There is a scene in a recent play in which a young man appears on stage with a deflated balloon which he tries to blow up. He tries and

41

tries, but for some reason he can't inflate it. A girl enters, takes the balloon, blows it up, ties it, returns it to its owner and departs. The young man looks sadly at the balloon, turns to the audience and says, "I had wanted to do it myself."

Blowing up the balloon is what, inadequately and inefficiently, the existing social service system has sought to do. Enabling the young man to blow it up himself is human development. To sustain the analogy, we would have had the young man apply for a balloon, submit to an interview in which we probed his reasons for requiring it then placed him on a waiting list. Ultimately, we would have delivered a pre-inflated balloon of different shape and colour than he had wanted — because the regulations required that these be standard — together with a set of instructions as to what he could and could not do with it, on pain of having it taken back if they were not followed. There is no element of human development in this approach, merely service delivery.

The human development approach would simply be to enable the young man to obtain the balloon, of whatever shape and colour he chose, and to provide for the availability of consultative service if, after trying to blow it up himself, he decided he wanted advice or assistance.

This very primitive analogy focuses the two approaches to social policy around which a polarization is today taking place, the service strategy and the income strategy.

Notwithstanding the existence of a certain number of income support programs, the existing structure is predominantly reflective of the service strategy. Proponents of the income strategy argue that we have now had thirty years of experience with this service strategy and its failure to combat poverty is clear. It is time to abandon it in favour of an income strategy. Defenders of the service strategy argue that it is not the strategy that has failed, only the attempt to carry it out on a totally inadequate shoestring.

There are two components to the newly evolving income strategy. The first is directed to individuals, the second to groups. Central to the income strategy as it relates to individuals is the concept of the guaranteed annual income. Central to the income strategy as it relates to groups is the concept of community control.

I won't deal at any length with the multitude of proposals that have been advanced for a guaranteed income, but they fall largely into two categories, those employing the negative income tax approach and those employing the social dividend approach. Within each of these categories there have been proposals made involving such varied levels of income guarantee and recovery rates on earned income, that cost estimates vary by many billions of dollars. The need, on the one hand, to maintain incentive to work by permitting retention of a substantial portion of earned income, and the need at the same time to keep expenditures to less than astronomical proportions are the two competing values. A number of guaranteed income tests are under way in the United States at present, aimed at discovering the effects on work incentive, life style, family relationships, etc., given various forms of income guarantee.

The guaranteed income represents the income strategy as it applies to individuals. The proposal, advanced by some proponents of the guaranteed income, that payments should be made wholly or partly in kind rather than in cash represents an attempt to graft the service strategy onto the income strategy. These people argue that the poor, as a result of the lifetime which has led to their present condition, are not equipped to cope with the sudden arrival of a guaranteed income. Instead they should be provided with food vouchers, clothing vouchers, etc. This thesis, whose paternalistic view of the poor is readily apparent, should either be demolished or confirmed by the results of the U.S. experiments in New Jersey, Wisconsin, Indiana and Washington.

It should also be noted with respect to the guaranteed annual income, that the contention that it would eliminate the need for any categorical or general assistance programs is not really true. If the income guaranty is set at either the poverty level of the lowest cost region in Canada or that of the national average, supplementation through some form of public assistance would still be required in high cost urban centers. Even if it were set nationally at the level required for high cost areas, or if different levels were set for each region reflecting living costs in those regions — which might tend to institutionalize regional disparities — there would still be the need of a supplementary assistance program to meet individual cases of special need.

However, the very strong argument advanced in support of the guaranteed income approach is that it liberates recipients from the debilitating effects of the supplications and investigations involved in obtaining public assistance. It is argued that a system which destroys dignity and threatens self-respect, while it may put bread on the table, cannot contribute to human development.

The second prong of the income strategy applies to groups and involves community control of services within the community. Horizontal organization of individual services would be largely replaced by vertical organization, with an integrated delivery system controlled by the local community and utilizing indigenous workers. Examples of this can be found in the United States in the Ford Foundation's Gray Areas Program, New York City's Mobilization for Youth program, the Community Action Programs of the Office of Economic Opportunity and the Model Cities Program.

What is involved in this approach is, in effect, the creation of a fourth level of government. The neighbourhood elects its own council which develops a program for neighbourhood service and which is provided with the funds to carry this program out. In the case of these American programs, multi-service centers have been established with personnel provided by government and private agencies becoming responsible to the executive director of the center who, in turn, is responsible to the neighbourhood council. As well, indigenous workers are hired as supportive personnel and a range of new services and community activities established in conjunction with the provision, under local control, of the traditional range of services.

This approach is being tried for the first time in Canada with the recent announcement of a joint funding by the Departments of National Health and Welfare and the Secretary of State of the program of the Black United Front of Nova Scotia. The Council of the Black United Front, to be elected by the black people of that province on a community-by-community basis, will develop a program of community activity for which the Federal Government will provide funds up to $100,000 in each of the next five years. The program will include such things as family life education, housing assistance, consumer economics and educational and job opportunities.

Having visited in Nova Scotia and seen the conditions of life of the black communities in that province, I can offer personal testimony that the traditional approach to service delivery has failed completely to reach these people. The hope is that the indigenous activation of the community can provide its members with what no program of government could, namely the self-confidence which

44

comes from discovering one's own capacities.

Labels are invariably over-simplifications and this is certainly true of the debate between the service strategy and the income strategy. Just as there has always been an income component to the present service system, so also there would need to be a service component to any system founded on an income strategy. The differences would lie in local control and individual choice with respect to these services.

An enormous number of experimental programs built around this income strategy are being tested in the United States. One of the most intriguing of these is an application of it to education. A number of experimental private schools have been established, each employing a different pedagogical approach but all of them differing from the more highly structured and disciplined approach offered by the public school system. Participating parents are provided with the funds to buy their children's education from whichever of the competing schools they feel offers the best product.

At first blush this seems a very radical departure from all our ideas of how education should be provided. But in fact, it differs from what presently exists in only two senses.

First, while private schools exist already as an alternative to the public schools, they exist only for the rich, who can afford the fees. Second, the market for these schools being limited to the rich, their pedagogical approach, internal organization and even admissions policy must be geared to the attitudes of this particular market.

Rather than being radical, this experiment really represents a return to the purest free enterprise concept — except that everyone is free to participate equally in the marketplace because each of the competing schools is within the financial reach of each of the consumers.

To properly carry out an income strategy will require a willingness on the part of government to spend a great deal of money in order to equalize opportunity for all. But this is not unique to the income strategy. It would also have involved a great deal of money had we ever determined to properly carry out a service strategy.

The full implementation of an income strategy as it applies to individuals, being centered on a guaranteed annual income, is clearly beyond the scope of provincial capacities. But short of this, there are many ways in which a province can adapt the programs which are within its jurisdiction to the philosophy underlying the income strategy.

The first and most obvious area is that of public assistance. Apart from those who fit into the special categories eligible for what is known as long-term assistance, a total disincentive to work is provided by the assistance cheque being reduced by the full amount of any earned income. Also, the holding of any form of full-time employment, however inadequate the income from it may be in relation to the needs of the family, is an absolute disqualification from receipt of any assistance.

If we are serious about injecting the goal of human development into this system, a progressive reduction rate on earned income must replace the 100 percent reduction rate which now applies, and the working poor made eligible to receive assistance where there is need.

Further, the definition of needs implicit in benefit levels must be expanded. Present allowances are inadequate to meet even the minimum requirements of food, clothing and shelter — although they purport to be designed to meet the range of human needs. There must be a recognition that to live as a man is more than just not being left to die. And this means provision of benefits sufficient to enable the recipient to function as a full member of the community.

These things will not happen as long as financially distressed municipalities are required to put up two dollars for every three dollars provided by the province for basic needs and to meet entirely the costs of special needs. The Federal Government already provides 50 percent of all these costs under the Canada Assistance Plan and would continue to do so for any expanded program. The Province of Ontario must, as the Province of New Brunswick has done, assume the full cost of the remaining 50 percent.

If we accept the provision of assistance to those who require it as a matter of their right and not our benevolence, then a system of appeal procedures must be designed to reflect the view of appellants as persons seeking redress for alleged violation of their rights, not supplicants seeking a more generous award of charity.

These things are basic to injecting the human development concept of the income strategy into our policies directed at individuals. Applying this strategy to groups, the key is a program of direct funding of citizens groups representative of disadvantaged communities. Indian communities are an obvious example, but urban poverty

46

communities are also in need of this approach. Costs of any such program would be shared by the Federal Government through the Canada Assistance Plan.

The Government of Ontario must encourage the participation of those it seeks to serve in the human development field by involving them in the making of the decisions which will affect their lives. This applies not only to the provision of community services, but also to such things as the planning of urban renewal and the creation of regional governments. Here again, the income strategy demands not token consultation but the provision of sufficient resources to the community affected to enable it to match the technical expertise with which big government has always managed to befuddle the little man.

This also applies to the creation of an Ontario counterpart of the new National Council of Welfare, with members representing welfare recipient organizations, tenant groups, Indian councils and other such organizations. And again, it must be provided with the resources necessary for well researched and documented advice, equal in technical expertise to that of government, but reflective of the attitudes of these "consumer" groups.

We are living in an era of unprecedented alienation and witnessing the emergence of a reaction to that alienation which is at the same time frightening and exciting. The powerless poor are banding together and asserting Poor Power. The powerless students are banding together to assert Student Power. The powerless Indians are asserting Red Power and the powerless blacks Black Power. It is what happened a half-century ago when the powerless workers banded together to form unions and assert Labour Power. It was a long and bloody struggle before we accepted Labour Power and adjusted our power structure accordingly. Even if our society were capable of surviving such a struggle again, fought this time on a dozen fronts simultaneously, surely we will not be so inflexible as to seek again to ride with General Motors rather than walk with the workers.

If we choose to man the barricades rather than share our power, then the next few years will be violent, frightening and bloody ones. But if we choose to welcome the rise of the downtrodden to claim their rightful share of what can be a good life for all, then the next few years will be among the most exciting and humanly productive we have ever known.

6

Poor Power
John Mooney

We don't want your damn money. We don't want your damn attitudes. We don't want your damn values. We want, and we are going to get, the power to control our lives. You know, the poor aren't only people on welfare. They are a minority of the poor. The poor are people who work very long hours for very low pay. More importantly, they do not have any control over their lives. The poor don't want money. Talk to a fellow on the street and ask him what he would think of a minimum income of $4,500 a year and he would say, "That is great." But because of his previous and present environment, he is not going to be aware of the fact that he is selling himself. If you don't offer an alternative, he is going to accept what the so-called experts propose. The solution to poverty is to let individuals run their own lives. It is not money but the sharing of power among people, poor people, middle class people.

The attitude that many people have that we have to do something for the poor people is wrong. We don't have to do anything for them. They'll do it themselves and they are doing it now. The Just Society movement has been organizing for several months. We have a corps of several hundred people who are attempting to organize the poor. The work is very difficult. But we are making progress. This is what we are doing. This is what we will continue to do until we have a strong enough power base to have a real say in what will happen to us and to the wealth of this province and this nation.

You were talking about parliamentary reform. The poor know it's not working. It's not working for the average Joe at all. It is not enough to modernize the parliamentary system. What you must do is change it so that poor people have a real say in the government of this country.

Poverty, like any other social ill, is a result of a given social structure of a given society. We are not ridding this country of poverty, and never will, as long as society assumes that poverty will continue to exist. Instead we are creating greater and more widespread poverty, and it is galloping. This is because of a social structure which has failed, in the name of democracy (to which I like to adhere), to satisfy these people. The welfare establishment contends that some type of guaranteed annual income is a necessity. To be sure, many poor would like a guaranteed income, but they are being led down the garden path. They are being led to self-destruction. Their dignity is being taken away from them by you people giving them a guaranteed income. It is an unrealistic approach. Money is not the answer to poverty.

They argue that social assistance—that is a nice name for welfare—will always be required as a safety net program. This assumes that poverty will continue to exist and that the poor will always be with us. You know that is a lot of crap! We, the poor, are of the opinion that welfare programs as they now exist are necessary only within the present structure and within the present system of attitudes of our society.

They even suggest that students should receive allowances to diminish the problem of dropouts. Give him enough money to go to school, and the kid will go to school. They assume that this is a major factor in kids dropping out of high school. Money will solve nothing, really. They need the money, but it is not a solution. Only when the system of ritual, rigidity, and formalization is abolished will the school dropout race cease.

In the area of taxation of family allowances, it is suggested that the well-to-do would continue to pay, or repay, 100 percent of the differential, and the poor would pay less than 100 percent, and when necessary the poor would pay nothing. A great system! But this too assumes that poverty will always be with us. But, more importantly, this device fosters division and resentment within society. From one sector of society, division and resentment is focused upon another sector. The low income worker thinks he is paying the shot for the welfare recipient. But he is not, he is paying the shot for the guy who is making $10,000 or $15,000 a year. The low income workers are paying the shot for tax free loans and forgiveable loans—not for bloody welfare. A very minuscule portion of this tax money goes into welfare.

Government at all levels, with the able assistance of advertising, uses phrases such as "welfare" and "social assistance" for one seg-

49

ment of society while for another sector of society it says the same thing with phrases such as "tax free loans" and "student awards". I was a student. I got welfare. But now it is called "student awards", "forgiveable loans", along with a host of other pleasant phrases for the consumption of you people. They all mean welfare! They all mean welfare!

Mr. Shifrin says some very nice things in his paper. And he says some things which need to be said, I suppose, from his position. However, what he says we have all heard before. We are well aware of what he says. What's more, he is probably much more aware of what is really needed than he has indicated. He has used words like radicalism and reconstruction, and has let us in on the earth-shaking news that government is responsible not only for radicalism, but for positive radicalism, and the obvious need for the restructuring of society, values and attitudes. I think we are aware of that to some extent.

However, it is what Mr. Shifrin does not say that is very interesting, very striking. Intentionally, or unintentionally, Mr. Shifrin has made his paper *appear* radical. We believe that this statement by Mr. Shifrin will certainly get a hell of a lot of votes, but it won't do anything to improve the present system.

Mr. Shifrin sees a real need. He talked around it and above it and under it, and he has come back where he began—a senior civil servant. Mr. Shifrin probably sees the reality, but sidesteps it, walks around it, etc., etc.

Mr. Shifrin urges the creation of what he calls a fourth level of government along neighborhood lines to facilitate a comprehensive workable system of neighborhood services. Funds for this would come from the Federal Government, and would be used for such things as family life, education, housing assistance, consumer education and job opportunities. He gives to this the name of "community control". Very radical! Except it is *not* community control. It bears no resemblance to community control. It is merely a superficial *facade* of community control.

This is simply an extension of the present paternal attitudes of government. You know, they allow the people to get involved. They allow the people to make insignificant decisions. It is nothing more than a "make work" program, because I have seen them in operation. He points out the example of New Jersey and the Federal grant to the Black United Front in Nova Scotia. Well, I will tell you what happened to the Ford Foundation's program in Newark, N.J. It was one of the first. When the people realized that they could control in a very, very, small way their lot, they attempted to exercise greater control along these lines. The United States Government, deciding it could not afford to subsidize what it believed to be revolution, cut off the funds. When the people in Nova Scotia begin to bang on government doors and shout, "We want more power and control over our lives", they too will find the government is suddenly short of money for further community activities.

The use of what is referred to as indigenous workers to affect change cannot be productive. Change will not take place when people are used by a government to facilitate nothing more than a better delivery service or expanded postal services.

Mr. Shifrin also suggests money will allow people to participate in education to a greater degree, but this is not true. They will not participate in education to a greater degree unless the people have control of education.

Finally, Mr. Shifrin tells us that government must show a willingness to spend a great deal of money in order to equalize opportunity. Money may help, but it is not the solution of the problem of the poor nor for many other people who are not poor. The question which I ask you is, Will government show a willingness to give the people the right to control their lives, to control their cities, and to control the national wealth of this nation? If you do not recognize and act upon the recognition that the people have a right to make decisions directly affecting not only their immediate needs but directly affecting all aspects of regional and national wealth, then you will be left behind. I don't know where you will be, but you will be left behind!

There are alternatives. There are real alternatives. We are aware of them, and many of us see the need for these alternatives.

7

Social Policy and Liberalism
James Trotter

The need for a new social policy for this province is desperately urgent. By the term "social policy" I do not mean some warmed-over hackneyed program of doling out vouchers for a few dollars to individuals in utterly hopeless circumstances.

The keystone of the Liberal social policy must be "the dignity of the individual". Whether we be small l or large L Liberals, we can look back on the role of Liberalism with some considerable pride in the contributions of Liberals to enhancing the "dignity of the individual". Liberalism of the eighteenth and more particularly of the nineteenth century made a tremendous contribution in throwing off the shackles of feudalism and establishing political democracy in that part of the world that we today, generally speaking, call the West. Liberal democracy had a tremendous drive and seemed to be the answer in a world of scarcity and want. Until about the beginning of the twentieth century no political or economic dogma has ever had such a wide appeal among the so-called masses.

We who have inherited Liberal democracy should by now be brutally aware that government in this province and in this country has not grasped the import of the great economic and social changes that are taking place and that have already taken place. We do not seem to be developing and exerting the resources within our people and in our country as we should and as we could. The initiative our system once had in world affairs has waned and could be lost unless we grasp the essentials of the changes that are taking place. And if we lose, personal freedom shall surely perish.

We should be most grateful to the past accomplishments of Liberalism. But let us use the past accomplishments of Liberalism and of Liberals as a guidepost and not as a hitching post. We would be indeed ungrateful if we did not acknowledge our debt to those who have gone before us. Our heritage has been obtained through a long and toilsome process. Perhaps the pioneers who laid the foundations of our society and of Liberalism laid them with instruments now out-of-date and by some methods that have become outmoded. But this does not detract from the lustre of their success. Rather it adds to it. With fewer and cruder instruments, with fewer opportunities to develop their abilities and to seek solutions to their problems than we have today, those who have preceded us have bequeathed to us the power of applied science and the idea of democracy.

It is the great challenge of our time to convince the world that democracy is more than just a counting of votes, and that applied science is to be used for programs for people, and not just for programming computers. Democracy has not yet found a sure way of providing all its citizens with an equal opportunity of sharing in the so-called affluent society. It has not yet succeeded in doing away with great social inequalities. But it contains within itself solutions for all these problems. And remember, no other known system offers a solution without at the same time demanding the fearful price of the sacrifice of personal liberty. Democracy alone offers the prospect of reconciling social progress with personal liberty.

Henry Ford had a great success in the Model T Ford. It was so successful that he refused to change it to any other model, despite the fact that competitors had introduced even better cars than the Model T. Not until the Ford Motor Company was surpassed by its competitors did it wake up and bring in the Model A.

It is the same with government. Unless a government meets the problems of the day with up-to-date knowledge, with zest and vigour, it too falls behind competing systems. We are failing to solve the problems of our day because we use old worn-out methods and theories that are no longer dynamic in the light of the history of the twentieth century. The result is there is great apathy on the part of many people toward public affairs. The young people particularly have shown disillusion with our society. Some of them have shown a tendency to want to "opt out" of our modern society. We Liberals want to "tune them in". But if we, as Liberals, are to "tune in" not only the young but people of all ages, including ourselves, we are going to have to come to grips with the problems of our day and age. Some economic beliefs held dearly by our grandfathers, which in our day are nothing but clichés, will have to be buried forever.

For example, in the days when our grandfathers lived in an economy of scarcity, they preached that "economic insecurity is essential for efficiency". In our day when production is a relatively minor problem, such jargon as "economic insecurity is essential for efficiency" is bunk. Of course, some will say that government action is interference with free enterprise and we should leave it all to the laws of demand and supply. Free enterprise is a sacred cow. We think that the Hindus have a strange belief when they allow sick cows to wander around spreading disease because to them the cow is sacred. The Hindu's belief is no more weird than ours if we sit idly by in the name of that sacred cow, "free enterprise", and permit untold hundreds of thousands of our fellow citizens to live blighted lives.

Twenty percent of our people live below what is called the poverty line. We must look for solutions that a few years ago would have been unthinkable, such as a guaranteed annual wage, the negative income tax and subsidized wages.

Our social legislation should be designed to prevent social breakdown in the individual, the family, or society as a whole. At all times the emphasis should be on prevention. Our social policy should be positive and constructive. Instead, today, it is designed to do a salvage job. At best our welfare legislation is nothing more than a jazzed-up version of the four-hundred-year-old Elizabethan poor laws. The prejudice is still widely held that most people receiving government assistance are bums and want to be on welfare. Anyone knowledgeable at all in social problems will tell you that such an utterance is a slander on the vast majority of the people receiving social assistance.

The displaced persons or "DPs" are not in camps in some far-off war-torn land, but they are here in Ontario. These are the people that automation has displaced because they are poorly educated, unskilled and mostly unemployable. Where is their dignity of the individual? These people are reduced to the deadly grind of poverty because governmental policies are either nonexistent or half-baked and infirm of purpose.

Seventy percent of working mothers are married to men earning less than $4,000 a year. Many thousands of mothers are the only support of their children. Yet the policy of the present provincial government in supporting day nurseries and day care centres has been one of almost wanton neglect.

At any given day and at any given time over half of the hospital

54

beds in this province and in this country are filled by people who are mentally ill. And yet, governments and the public generally are shamefully complacent in the treatment and in the prevention of mental illness. It has been estimated that over half a billion dollars a year is lost to the Canadian economy because of mental illness. Mental illness is one more problem that we are going to have to attack because of urbanization. When it is remembered that the Government of Ontario spends approximately $22.20 per day on each inmate in our provincial and district jails, $40.50 per day for a general hospital patient and approximately $13.12 per day per patient on the treatment of the mentally ill, it can hardly be expected that sufficient skilled personnel or adequate buildings can be provided. The Ontario Hospital at 999 Queen Street has been given a new name. It is now called the Queen Street Mental Health Centre. But despite the new name and modernized front, it is still the same, old bastille that was built many years before Confederation. We Liberals will not tolerate modern fronts and fancy new names that only serve to cover up festering problems.

The term "social policy" involves far more than just an adequate income, important as that is. The dignity of the individual can only be enhanced if his quality of living is enriched. In this regard the challenge of the urbanization of our society poses our most difficult problem. By 1980 one-third of all of Canada's population will live in three cities, Montreal, Toronto and Vancouver. As the early pioneers of this country were faced with the challenges of the frontier, our generation is faced with the challenges of the "urban frontier".

Because of the mass movement to urban centres, untold hundreds of thousands of people will spend most of their lives as tenants in huge building complexes. Under our present landlord and tenant laws, a tenant is at the mercy of the landlord. A tenant in a large apartment complex has a status similar to a serf's in feudal times. Certainly our landlord and tenant law must be drastically revised. But more than that, our social policy in dealing with the great apartment complexes and with urban redevelopment needs a new direction. At the present time these huge apartment complexes are like monstrous filing cabinets of steel and concrete where people are filed away. They emphasize what is happening to the individual in our modern society which is, in so many cases, that the individual feels a complete alienation from any sense of personal power over his own life. The great impersonal city is swallowing him to such an extent that he is cut off from the community in which he lives. The individual is robbed of his personality and denuded of his self-esteem.

Government policy should be so directed as to encourage and nurture a community spirit. The modern shopping plaza can become the new town hall for a meeting place. Personal involvement by the individual is the only way for a healthy, socially minded, animated society. Tenants' associations, ratepayers' associations and similar organizations must be encouraged to give the individual an opportunity to exercise some power over his own destiny.

These, then, are but a few of the problems that must be solved. Let us go forth eager to implement social policies that are meaningful and relevant to challenges of the 1970s.

8

An Urban Strategy for an Urban Ontario
John Parkin

Architecture (like politics) is a social art in the service of man and committed to human betterment. There may be architects who believe that they are artists in the sense that painters and sculptors are artists; that their concerns are exclusively form, texture and colour. They are wrong. They are avoiding their responsibility and attempting to escape from urban reality. If cures are to be found for the urban migraine which has beset our nation, architects cannot remain unconcerned.

The architect has, after all, some things in common with the politician. Lobbying is an occupational hazard for both. Apathy is the normal climate in which both appear to work. There are no second prizes for either — one builds or one governs. The alternatives are to simply observe or to criticize. (And when one stops building or stops governing it is, as the late Hon. C.G. Power once said, "but a short step from the private car to the upper berth".)

We are, in fact, sitting on an urban time bomb. The urban reality which faces us is an inventory of mediocrity, blight, congestion, pollution, alienation and increasing urban disturbance. Today, about one-third of the world's three billion people live in urban areas. By the year 2000 (only thirty years away) more than 60 percent of an estimated six billion population will be urbanized.

In these terms, Canada (indeed all of North America) is urbanized now. The population of our eleven largest cities is over eight million and has increased at twice the rate of growth of the remainder of Canada (10.4 percent as opposed to 5.2 percent). Two-thirds of the population of Canada lives in communities of more than 100,000 and 80 percent in communities of over 30,000. While we have not yet reached the position of the United States, where 70 percent of the urban population is concentrated on 1 percent of the total land area, we are well on our way. For example, in fifteen years the area from Niagara Falls to Oshawa will be one giant urban complex.

While the city itself is 5,000 years old, the metropolis is a new phenomenon, no more than 100 years old. A few population concentrations, however, already exceed present metropolitan concepts and are now more properly termed megalopolitan. In fifty years, the majority of the world's population may well be accommodated in vast megalopolises, each with populations of 20 million or more.

The city merges into the metropolis, and the metropolis into the megalopolis. This pattern is already becoming identifiable. The spread from Boston to Washington, a continuous urban form planners term a "conurbation", is the wealthiest, most industrialized area in the world. Other examples include Milwaukee to Chicago to Cleveland, or San Diego to well north of Los Angeles. This new phenomenon in the history of society has implications so vast that one scholar described it as giving one "the feeling of looking at the dawn of a new stage in human civilization".

The population explosion and rapid urban growth have been accompanied by a technological explosion. The range and variety of materials and systems available to architects and engineers today offer limitless possibilities to suit any building purpose. And the environment—thermal, visual and acoustical—can be controlled to meet practically any design criteria.

The incredible expansion of construction can be described most graphically by the fact that every object in North America must be doubled between now and the year 2000. For every expressway that now exists another must be built in the next thirty years. For every building, house or machine, there must be another building, house or machine built within that time. It has taken nearly 400 years to create the physical "plant" that is North America today. In the next thirty years it must be doubled.

The measure of the success we achieve in the remaining years of this century is of critical importance in the survival of our species. The issue of "How will man live?" is second only in importance to "Will man live?". We have often been described as the only species which will foul its own nest. We have been obsessed with quantity and only incidentally concerned with quality. So far, man has gone on the assumption that men, women and children are almost infinitely plastic, provided they get certain minimal amounts of water, food, light, space and air. Little thought, and less experimentation, has been directed to the quality of the space in which man lives.

Clearly, sweeping and fundamental changes are required in the decision-making techniques forming our cities—if, indeed, there ever were any conscious decision-making processes at work. The nature and form of our environment is capable of being controlled. The question is: Are we willing to bring collective pressure to bear on the problems inhibiting the achievement of man's optimal environment? This must be done by governments, but ironically one of the principal impediments to the renewal of cities appears to be partly overgovernment and partly absence of government.

Indeed, we are overgoverned, at least in the sense of being overcrowded with governments. Besides the 1 federal, 10 provincial and 2 territorial governments, there are 4,866 municipal jurisdictions—a total of almost 5,000 governments. Only the 4,866 multipurpose municipalities are specifically charged with the task of dealing with urban detail. Many of the municipalities verge on bankruptcy, with the principal decisions affecting them being made by the senior and absentee levels of government. Several of the more populous provinces, in fact, appear to fear the potential political power of their major metropolitan areas far more than they fear the power of the federal government. It is politically expedient for the provinces to ignore many of the major urban problems of their municipalities for fear of losing real power to the cities.

Unfortunately, the senior levels of government often make decisions affecting cities and towns without fully understanding the physical consequences. Provincial governments build highways or establish commuter train services, install major utility services, build houses, provide electricity, erect their own plants and buildings, and determine or greatly influence many other factors, including centres of higher education. Together, the province's actions go a long way towards determining the broad outline of development in any region. At the same time, the federal government builds harbours, airports, buildings, and regulates railways and pipelines. All of these have a great impact on our cities.

The municipalities are at the receiving end, playing a dual role. First, they have to provide basic services to the community: the roads, water and drainage that service property directly. Second, they are expected to coordinate the activities of all three levels of government, to say nothing of those of the private sector. The municipality is asked to take the responsibility of planning its area when it has no jurisdiction over the vital actions of many departments and agencies of the provincial and federal governments and has only limited means of guiding private development. Even the school boards within its territory are beyond its reach. Municipalities are thus reduced to making partial plans to cope with an unpredictable future.

In view of the significant function of municipal government in our country, is it not ironic that our constitutional discussions are centred almost totally on the relationship between the federal and provincial governments to the exclusion of the nearly 5,000 governments to whose care is entrusted the urban dweller? The rationale used to justify this neglect is that urban renewal and city change are properly provincial and primarily local functions, according to current interpretations of the British North America Act, and therefore not federal functions at all. If the BNA Act is responsible for this anomaly, perhaps it should be amended.

If the constitutional conferences in the immediate future fail to address themselves to local and urban problems and disparities, as well as to federal-provincial constitutional abstractions, the consequences might well be serious for the 70 percent of this nation's population who live in cities.

The nation's festering problems are urban concerns—inadequate housing, mass transportation, crowded educational facilities, lack of recreational outlets, pollution, poverty, and so on. The level of government that first tackles and solves these urban problems will inherit the authority that counts in deciding the future of this land. Human ingenuity and human will *can* solve the problems we face. We must mount an attack on the urban problem. We must defuse this time bomb.

In theory, Ottawa is scarcely allowed to acknowledge the existence of our 4,866 incorporated municipalities, for the British North America Act gave the provinces exclusive power over municipal institutions. In practice, however, through an increasing system of grants to the provinces for various municipal programs, the reality of "junior" governments is, in fact, recognized. What is lacking at the federal level is an integrated coordinated program of attack on urban problems—our federal Department of Urban Affairs?

Such a department should be created and charged with interrelating federal aid in the fields of housing, poverty, pollution and transportation.

Much of the foment and action in Canada has passed from Ottawa to the provincial capitals. Not only are the provinces now spending as much collectively as the federal government, but they are spending in areas of more immediate human concern: education, health and social welfare. Their spending, however, lacks coordination.

In Ontario, for example, there is a Department of Municipal Affairs whose administrative business is the affairs of some 500 municipalities, many of them small. But the Minister of Municipal Affairs does not hold a brief when the departments of welfare, education and health bring down new regulations which the cities must implement and finance. Obviously, there is an inherent conflict in the purposes of local government.

The proliferation of provincial boards and agencies, from some of which there is little practical appeal, must be checked. Surely there is no excuse for the existence of boards whose decisions cannot be appealed through the courts.

The need is not for tighter, more authoritative control, but for a clarification of the purposes and duties of local government in an urban age. We need a provincial Department of Urban Environment to deal with all aspects of city life.

Crown corporations, agencies and government boards make countless design decisions daily on all levels, often without realizing it. When the Saskatchewan Power Corporation decides underground wiring is a luxury the consumer must pay for, when the Canadian Broadcasting Corporation contemplates a production facility not in accord with the best principles of planning, when public buildings are located without appropriate thought given to their beneficial influence on renewal, when cultural centres are wrongly thought of as slum clearance projects, then government fails in its understanding of planning issues.

The Canadian National Railway, on the other hand, has in recent years, and in all forms of design, fulfilled a unique leadership role. From a provocative symbol and imaginatively designed rolling stock through to notable contributions to the urban cores of Edmonton and Montreal, CN presents a distinguished example of enlightened corporate design patronage.

Taxation should be used to encourage better planning performance. Both local property tax and federal income tax can be adapted to reward the man who maintains his property. Assessment should

61

encourage, rather than discourage, good architecture. Tax incentives should be created to encourage those who provide open land, plazas, arcades or development rights for public use. The tax lever should be used on those who pollute air, land and water, with remissions when the offending source is removed.

New concepts of assessment are urgently required. Assessment should be heavily weighted against land and lightened on buildings. Most present assessment discourages quality development, and results in underdevelopment. Parking lots and shoddy "taxpayers" abound.

We have an excellent National Building Code of Canada backed by the resources of the National Research Council. We must adopt this code nationally, for none of our municipalities have comparable means at their disposal to adapt, test and modify code requirements. Yet some of our cities prefer an independent course and permit their officials arbitrary discretionary interpretation of their codes. The resulting chaos confuses not only would-be homeowners, but builders as well.

There is no budget for urban research worthy of the name though millions are spent yearly on farm, forestry and fisheries research. Worthy as all these programs are, they are product-oriented not people-oriented.

According to a report in *Time* magazine the social sciences get less than 3 percent of U.S. federal research money, while "there is always plenty of money available from almost any foundation for cardiac disease and cancer research".*

The scale of urban development is so immense, and our ignorance of cause and solution so vast, that we shall need the simultaneous perhaps competitive research of many minds in many institutions— public and private, profit and non-profit—to even begin to understand the human problem and to project answers.

Men may find God in nature, but when they look at cities they are viewing themselves—and what we see mirrored in our cities these days is not very flattering. Resource control, conservation and pollution control could be a practical demonstration of cooperative federalism. We Canadians should demand of our legislatures effective control of land use, air, water, noise and even visual abuse.

Water control, the politics and strategy of water management, has

* *Time*, March 17, 1967, p. 68.

been the basis of civilization since history began. In Canada we only dimly apprehend water politics, despite the fact that we possess one quarter of the world's supply of fresh water. We North Americans are on our way to putrefying every major river system by unchecked dumping of raw human sewage, pesticides, detergents, and industrial chemicals and wastes. We are indeed the effluent society!

The dynamics of a national-regional water transportation-distribution system could enable us to support a vastly greater population over a greater geographic area. Our water resources are our most valuable Canadian asset. Unlike certain of our other natural resources we own 100 percent of our water potential—or do we?

> Just go out for a breath of air,
> And you'll be ready for Medicare.*

Air pollution is so vast a problem that it has inspired mostly apathy. Some of our cities have no pollution control laws at all, and laws elsewhere are for the most part weak, archaic or unenforced. Expert advice suggests that 50 cents per head per year would keep most cities in Canada reasonably clean—more, apparently, than most Canadians are prepared to pay.

Federal and provincial governments must be made to recognize that integrated urban transportation systems are a shared responsibility. Our cities face a traffic jam expected to at least double in twenty years. There is undoubtedly a point of saturation, probably at the ratio of one car for every person who can drive. Growth of the automobile population, therefore, will be tied to and limited by the growth of human population, as great as that may be. Building roads for this controlled total is at least a definable, if enormous, job.

Our transport habits have changed in the past fifteen years with the move of industry and homes from city centres. No one transportation mode—cars, buses, subways or commuter trains— can handle all the traffic growth that is forecast. Achieving the correct mix is the essence of an integrated transportation policy. The cost of providing the necessary variety of transportation modes and the size of the areas to be covered are obviously beyond the scope of any one government level.

Most of the preceding discussion has concerned statistical, stra-

* "Pollution", Tom Lehrer.

tegic and political matters. But a nation of urban excellence cannot be built without consideration of matters of subjective judgment. We ought, as Canadians, to pursue a higher quality of public art.

We must complete a national inventory of historic buildings and landmarks. When we have identified those buildings of true value, let us create a "National Trust" to maintain them. Let us permit their owners lifetime occupancy on condition that the buildings be deeded to the state. We all accept the validity of our need to establish and maintain national parks and herds of bison in the wilderness. Why not extend this concept to the heart of our cities? Why not provincial parks for cities?

Where buildings are concerned, let us be very sure that sentiment does not cloud our desire for real quality. History is constantly in the making. Time may prove that what is being built today is superior to our inherited architecture. Cities are organic living things; they have never been immutable in their form. Our older buildings were valid in their time, but does the space occupied by some of them fulfill today's highest purpose? Toronto's old city hall is a case in point. Urban space—and buildings are but urban space—is to be lived in, as well as looked at. While cities must not be allowed to sacrifice their architectural heritage, they cannot become mere museums. Cities, after all, are where the action is.

The same thoughts apply to sculpture. Not only is it radially expressive of our age, but it is capable of probing the future. The rights of the minority elite who studiously and sincerely are devoted to contemporary art should be as respected as any other minority right. In fact, they should be as respected as the more obvious rights of the majority. It should be possible for a civic body to purchase a piece of contemporary sculpture for a public building without the irresponsible jeering that accompanied the purchase of the Henry Moore for Toronto's Nathan Phillips Square.

A percentage of the cost of all buildings should be devoted to the arts. To ensure that that percentage is wisely spent, the choice must be left to the judgment of the thoughtful and informed few. In short, we must preserve all that is worthy from our past public art, while encouraging the best in our present and future public art.

One of my favourite urban guidelines appears on a street sign in Edinburgh.

The Amenity of our Streets is recommended to your care.

64

Not only our streets, but all the worthy elements and details of our cities are recommended to your care.

9

City Power
Colin Vaughan

John C. Parkin's paper, "An Urban Strategy for an Urban Ontario", mirrors too much of what has been said at too many political conferences in the past. Many of these proposals were made in 1960 at the Kingston Conference. They were repeated vociferously—and I was one of those repeating them—at the National Liberal Conference in Ottawa in 1966. However, we are now entering the 1970s and we cannot make them any more. Their time is past—they are too timid, they are too much an extension of the present art, they are too full of the conventional wisdom.

The most significant point that the Parkin paper fails to recognize is the strength and the power of the cities. This is also the one point that has been ignored completely by our legislators, whether they be provincial, federal or municipal. If you, the members of the Liberal Party, do not sense the change that is occurring in the cities of North America and spreading to other cities throughout the world—God help you! The manifestation in the streets of our cities is a flexing of the urban muscle. The cities will become a power unto themselves and the period is ending when the cities are considered the "poor children" of the provinces and the federal government.

We see it all around us every day. We see the anarchy of the poor and dispossessed. We see the revolutionary challenges of youth, of students, of communities in the cities. In the terms of traditional politics, the age of reason has ended. Your task as a political party is to decide whether the forces that are moving in the city are going to be creative or destructive, evolutionary or revolutionary. It is as simple as that.

A totally new philosophy is required, one which recognizes that the cities exist, that the cities are powerful and that the strength of the nation depends on the health of the cities. We see the emergence of the powerful regional city, the megalopolis that the Parkin paper mentions, and with it urban governments which are beginning to

66

transcend and challenge the provinces and the nation in terms of economy, employment, productivity and exports. The cities are becoming mini-nations engaged in the development and export of information and skill, the abilities needed to unleash the forces of technological and social change. These forces are becoming more critical day by day for the existence of the society we are creating. They are becoming much more important than rural produce, for these are the skills that get us from the earth to the moon. These are the skills which will liberate both urban and rural man.

The Parkin paper starts with an excellent summary of the problem. I cannot agree with it on the responsibilities of the professions. The professions, in most respects, have failed in attacking the problems of the cities. Their members live in isolated clubs and are remote from the reality of the streets. They have used their political power for the expansion of their own interest but have yet to use this power effectively for the common good.

As an example, my architectural firm has recently been involved in the introduction of a building system for educational facilities in Metropolitan Toronto. This system is a beginning, the very first step, in the use of advanced industrial technology in meeting the problems of the city. It will enable the users of a building to respond to their own needs through the technology of a building system. It is the first truly industrial rationalization of the building industry. Although the Parkin firm is one that has supported this move, one of the greatest roadblocks to this new technology in its early stages was the architectural profession. They choose to stand between a rationalized industrial process and the people who would use it. It is fortunate for those outside the professions that the elected representatives in Metropolitan Toronto have resisted its reaction and have proceeded with the introduction of the building system.

The Parkin paper goes on to analyze the conventional statistics of the "urban time bomb" and the governmental crisis. But having undertaken this analysis, two suggestions are then made which have proven ineffective in the city. The first is that we must have a federal Department of Urban Affairs. It really doesn't matter. He then suggests a provincial Department of Environmental Affairs. It really doesn't matter.

In effect, these units already exist other than in name—at the federal level we have the CMHC—and other government agencies; in

67

the province we have a Department of Municipal Affairs and the Ontario Housing Corporation. I believe that the institutionalization of federal and provincial departments centralizes power, removing it further from the cities and isolating it further from the people. Needed is a decentralization of the bureaucracies, not more and more centralization. Centralization will worsen the malaise of having decisions made by remote bureaucrats isolated from the reality of the streets. Decentralization will bring about a direct interface between people and their governments.

Sadly lacking in the Parkin paper is any understanding of the organization of the political power of the city itself We in the cities are not the children of the Federal Government, nor of the provincial governments. We are more than 70 percent of Canada in people, in productivity, in skill—in every respect. Until we flex our muscle and make the nation realize that we are the reason that it exists, the cities will always be the poor children and unable to meet their needs.

The paper then refers to the need for taxation to encourage better performance. Surely, all we have to do is grow wheat in the city and all our problems will disappear. Wheat seems to be the key for making demands of the federal government and for assuring the prosperity of certain regions of this country. We do not have wheat in the cities, so our strength is drained off to satisfy other regional demands. The paper ignores one of the greatest problems, which is taxation for the reacquisition of land so that it may be used to satisfy community needs rather than private interests. The rights to the resources of air and water are well established, but the right to the resource of land is not. We have no control over the development of our land—it is in private ownership and exploited for private gain. The taxation which would be useful would be directed at reacquiring the land of this continent and putting it back in the hands of the people, where it was over a hundred years ago. If this direction is not followed in the immediate future, massive land nationalization will have to take place in order to rationalize the development of the expanding cities.

The paper then deals with urban research—urban research must be directed through action. Research in the social sciences, resource control and transportation systems is not enough. These fields are currently the responsibilities of other levels of government and the responsibility must be given back to the cities. If they are not *given* back then they must be *taken* back and implementation must become the first priority—not research. Research produces paper—action produces results which can be tested and evaluated as a basis for further action. Fundamental to the increased research in social sciences is a presumption that research workers—sociologists, social workers, psychologists—are better able to speak for communities than are the communities themselves. Recently I was confronted by a sociologist, representing an apartment developer, who informed a government board how I live, how many children I have and described the life style of the community in which I live. In every case he was wrong— but it is this misinformation which is used to make planning and social decisions affecting the lives of human beings. The need is for social action centred on the people to be served, not social research for the support of the smugness of experts.

The problem of water pollution in Toronto is not related to what the United States is doing; rather it is related to what Chicago and Detroit are doing. It is this relationship of one city to other cities that is important. As soon as a city recognizes that it is the one caus- ing the pollution and is affected by the pollution of other cities, the sooner it will be in a position to deal with its own problems and the sooner the problem will be solved—in the field, not in a research laboratory.

Finally, the Parkin paper mentions non-material evaluation—the evaluation of the environment—"by the thoughtful and informed few". This is the greatest weakness of the whole paper. This philosophy permeates the paper from the beginning. It says, let us increase the power of the Federal Government, let us increase the power of provin- cial government, let other governments administer the cities. The problem already facing the cities is that "the thoughtful and informed few" are making the decisions for the "uninformed" many, and this is the underlying reason why there is trouble in the cities.

What is required is an opposite philosophy and if you are to survive as a political party you must recognize this. The new philo- sophy will not direct power upwards to the few but downwards to the many. Power must flow from the federal government and from the province to the cities and to the people who live in the cities. These people must have the right to direct their own lives, to admin- ister their own school systems, to decide how their children will grow up, how land will be used, how to solve the problems of pollution and transportation. They must have the power to deal with those who are now raping the urban environment.

The Federal Government and the Provincial Government have failed. It is now up to city states to take over and determine their own ends. That is the crux of it—we must put the power, the decision making process, the technology, the art, into the hands of the people. Otherwise, it will be the fascism of the "thoughtful and informed few" who control us through the concentration of power into too few hands. We will not succeed in the cities until we give power in its own right to the people so that they may decide for themselves.

The political party which recognizes the cities as a political force will be unpopular with those who live outside the metropolitan areas. Nevertheless, the draining off of the city's vitality to the satisfaction of irrelevant, nationalistic and provincial goals must stop. Without the strength and prosperity of the cities, none of the other goals will be met, nor would the nation exist.

The cities are already challenging the validity of nationalism and provincialism, both here and in the United States. They are challenging the inadequacies of the goals of the nation and of the provinces—these goals are irrelevant to the needs of the cities. The cities will continue to grow as centres, as regional political units and the nation must recognize city power. If it refuses, we may have to deal with city separatism.

We must deal with reality. The cities are the power and prosperity of the nation. The Parkin paper tells you what you should have done yesterday. As a political party your task is to decide what must be done for tomorrow.

10

A Housing Policy for Ontario
Paul Hellyer

Unfortunately, it is impossible to formulate a single housing policy to meet all of the needs of the entire country or of any province. The Task Force on Housing and Urban Affairs that I headed found this to be true. There was no single solution—some solutions would help some people in some parts of Canada; some solutions were more universally applicable, but a whole range of changes was needed to accomplish the type of improvement that we had in mind.

There are, however, some policies which are common to all parts of Ontario. First of all, the question of interest rates applies universally. It is just as important to the farmers, to the people in the small villages and the small towns, as it is to people in large cities. This is basically an economic problem, but it is going to have to be solved. If it is not solved in the next two or three years, we shall have to adopt some general policy of interest rate subsidization. To do so would be an admission of utter defeat in our economic policy.

Second, the availability of money is universally a problem. This is true at the present time when capital is short all over the world—Canada is no exception. There are so many things to do and so many demands for savings that the supply of funds is particularly difficult in the outlying regions, in the farming areas, in the small towns and villages of our province. I think our great financial institutions could improve their record in these areas. The Task Force found that our centralized institutions, which have done such a good job in some respects, were not fully aware of their responsibility to plough back into some of the smaller centres, something comparable to the savings that were collected there. Consequently, we recommended that either this be done or some new form of financial institution be developed which would make available to the people in smaller centres their share of their own savings.

Now we know that this can be done. Amongst the people that I interviewed when I was in Europe were a number of bankers in Norway. There they have a banking system which is not too different from our own, but they make a special point of ensuring that in the northern regions of that country an amount of money comparable to what they have collected in savings and deposits is made available for investment. So, it can be done. I would hope that our financial institutions would accept the responsibility for a similar policy here and only leave to government the problems of residual lending. Lending is a market operation, and best performed by the market. But government should be ready, willing and able to step in and meet particular needs in particular areas from time to time when, for one reason or another, funds are not available from ordinary market sources.

The third universal problem is the absence of a building code. There is just no reason why we could not have a province-wide building code. Built into it, of course, there could be provisions which would take into account regional differences—because there are some legitimate regional differences. But all these differences could be encompassed within one overall code.

I often use the example of the automobile. If you had to have different sized wheels and tires for every municipality and different windshields, for example, think of how outrageous the cost of cars would be. It would be totally impossible for a workingman to have an automobile. Yet, somehow, automobiles have been standardized. In the building field, and particularly in housing, on the other hand, we have no standardization, thereby making it impossible to get the kind of savings that are possible through standardization. I speak with some experience in this field for I once built in four different municipalities in Toronto at approximately the same time, and had to cope with four different building codes. Everything had to be done differently. It was a nightmare of red tape and confusion, and at extra cost, which is the thing that we are most concerned about.

These are some of the things we can do. The main housing problem of the future however is really a problem of the great cities.

The process of urbanization is inexorable. It is happening, it is going to happen, and there is nothing we can do to stop it. In every

72

country I visited, the same comment was made—"There is a regional problem". It is caused, basically, by people leaving the rural areas and moving into the larger centres. It is happening, not just in Canada, not just in North America, but in most parts of the world. It is a function of an irresistible technological change, and, therefore, to try and stop it—although you can ameliorate it perhaps to a certain extent—is something like putting your hand against the dyke when you know the dam is about to burst.

Perhaps, by way of an aside, I might say that no country that I have visited yet has had an accurate measurement of the total economic cost of relative policies in this field. In other words, no one has made an attempt to measure the social capital cost that they were trying to save in one area, against the extra economic cost of regional development, or trying, in effect, to turn the clock back. This would be a good exercise for someone—to find out just precisely what the measurable values are. After that the political judgments—the subjective judgments—could be added.

People want to be where the action is. In a city you can maximize the opportunities, or you can maximize the contact that you make for minimum cost. This way the things you want, whether they are in the field of education or recreation or of job opportunities are most likely to be available to you.

At the same time, this mass migration creates many problems because the cities and their governments were not designed to cope with this kind of growth. As a matter of fact, most of them were not designed at all. Some of them had street patterns laid out years ago by perfectly qualified Ontario land surveyors. You can see evidence of that. Yonge Street, for example, is intersected by King and Queen and College, and so on, and that is all very neat and tidy. But no one had time to foresee what the Toronto of today, let alone the Toronto of ten or twenty years from now, might look like. Consequently, you have a central core which is not designed to cope with all of the functions of the total system, and this creates a multitude of interacting and very complex problems—pollution, strangulation of traffic, excessive noise, and so on.

There are three or four structural changes taking place which have a great influence on city development. First is the form of city government. The Task Force found that there was not a single major urban centre in Canada that had what we thought was the right structure of government. Now it is easy to say that what we have is wrong; it is perhaps a little more difficult to say what would work more effectively. In principle, however, city government should have the overall responsibility for land use planning of the entire urban area. It should be responsible for transportation and the essential services as well as the other things that either make or break a great city. It should have the power to delegate downward to much smaller segments some of the individual decisions that have to be made. It is obvious that you cannot govern a great city like New York and make decisions at the central level affecting local detail—whether the swimming will be coeducational on Saturday afternoon; whether someone should be allowed to convert the third story of their house by installing a sink so their in-laws can live with them. This kind of decision is really not a function of a central government—whether it is a city government or a state government. This kind of decision must be delegated right down the line, more than we do at the present.

But, similarly, you cannot have six different boroughs, or six different divisions, making decisions about the ultimate shape, size and complexion of a great urban centre. The only comforting thing I have found was that this problem is not unique to Canada, and that we are probably about as far advanced as anyone. In Brussels, for example, I found they have nineteen municipalities and, literally, a situation where you have a firehall on one side of the street, and a fire on the other, and they come no closer together than visually because that is the way the municipal structure is set up. The present structure of city government, therefore, is a real restraint on development and planning.

The second and related constraint is the transportation system. We have not yet adapted our thinking to the technological revolution caused by the automobile. This, too, is a function of—dare I say it—the basic conservatism of man. This is what the argument on the unification of the Armed Forces was all about. The technological revolution of the last thirty years had overtaken the institutional changes. Similarly, the automobile has had an impact on our cities. We have not yet really thought through what kind of transportation systems we should have in order to move millions of people from one part of the city to another with relative ease and comfort. This must be done if we are going to regain some of the quality of life we think is now slipping away.

The third constraint is inadequate financing. Municipalities have to have adequate financing in order to operate. I have found that some of the countries that I visited are much more progressive than others in this field. An example of our problem was presented to the Task Force by the Borough of Scarborough. Their presentation made crystal clear that they would not permit a workingman's house, i.e. a small house, to be built because of its effect on the tax structure. It is ridiculous to let the tax structure determine the physical shape of a city and the kind of accommodation that is available for people when housing has such a profound effect on the quality of life.

Finally, and related to land use planning and the structure of government, municipalities have to get into the land development business. I am completely convinced of that. The Task Force took a very strong position on it, a position which has come under attack from many quarters largely because it took on such a large group of vested interests. But there is just no way—and this has been substantiated by my studies in Europe this summer—that you can keep land costs down and get the benefits both of adequate planning and of reasonable prices for new housing, unless land development becomes a function of municipal governments. For myself, I do not believe that land development should be a function of the provincial government. The provincial governments are in the business, but they muck up everything. Every time I see a Toronto newspaper that proclaims "Malvern to go ahead", I recall seeing that headline three years ago, or was it six years ago, or was it eight years ago, or was it ten years ago—it could have been fifteen years ago. The federal-provincial partnership bought that land in 1953 to try to hold down soaring land prices in Toronto—and it still is not developed. It is supposed to be going ahead now; I would like to take a good look at the project when it is completed to see what it will be like.

Talk about failure to use a principle to advantage—that was it. Yet, even in 1953, we knew what could be done, and at that time land prices were reasonable. That land was bought for an average price of about $1,000 per acre and at that time land much closer to town could have been bought for the same amount of money. Immediately after the war, some of the best prime land in the City of Toronto was priced at $400 per acre. If municipalities had gone into the land business then, you could still build a workingman's house

75

today for $20,000. But you cannot and never will be able to do it again in Toronto.

Although the constraints I have described are fundamental and structural, we are still only treating symptoms rather than basic causes. One of the consequences of this structural rigidity is the tendency to build an increasingly larger proportion of high rise dwellings. Now, I have nothing against high rise. I think that people should be allowed their personal choice. I have an apartment in Toronto, and it suits my requirements very well. But every time the whole family is there for about forty-eight hours, we almost go up the walls. When they are all finished university, and living away from home, I am sure it will be completely adequate. There is a time in people's lives when apartment living is fine. For example, when you are young, when you have no children, and when you are older and your children only come and see you when they need money, or on special holidays and occasions like that. Some people like indoor gardening, and hanging boxes over the railing; more power to them. I believe in freedom of choice. People should be allowed to live in apartments if they want to. What I really do not like, though (and I feel very, very strongly about this), is *dictating* to future generations that they must raise their families in these vertical filing cabinets.

As you know, I am not a wild theorist. I have some practical knowledge in this area, and I know that we can do better. We can provide a broader range of choice. Most Canadians would prefer this. The Task Force found that about 90 percent of the people who had families under sixteen or seventeen years of age wanted a plot of land of their own. Whether it was to be town housing, single family, duplex, quadruplex, or something else, they wanted something they could call their own. They wanted their own property so that the kids could go out and play in the mud and plant some petunias and build a fort and do the kinds of things they like without having the superintendent come along and take a baseball bat to them.

This requirement for privacy and space is a deeply inbred need. It is not just characteristic of Canadians. We often look at what the Swedes do and suggest that if we could only copy them, all would be well. I have just been in Sweden where a recent poll showed that 85 percent of their people with families want accommodation on the ground; they do not like the high rises either. Nevertheless, many high rises are being built in Sweden because they have the same kind of structural problems that we have, which they have not solved either. It has been recently shown that the suicide rate is several times higher above the fifth floor. My complaint is that we build these high rise apartments not because anyone says they are good, not because people want them, not because they are the solution to human problems, not because they are going to emancipate our people and contribute to the quality of life for the next generation, but because we drift with the tide.

But I want to pose a thesis, which you will hear more about in the next year or two, and that is that most policies are reactions to historical events rather than clearly thought out logic. I used to say "some" policies, but, the more I move around and the more people I talk to, the more I say "most" major policies are reactions to historical events. In other words, you have a fire, you have a depression, you have a war, you have a flood, you have a famine, and somebody reacts to it. A policy is adopted and some years later people say, "What did you do that for?" One very bright, articulate Danish civil servant, an excellent administrator, put it this way: "At least, if you have a snowstorm, you know what to do." Well, this is right, but is it good enough? Too often, when we know the structure is not right, when we know the form of government is not right, and we know inadequate consideration has been given to transportation systems, we just muddle along. We do not have the initiative, the imagination and, perhaps, in some cases, the political courage to eliminate the structural rigidity.

We copy each other tremendously. There is a conventional wisdom which is international. We do many of the same things that they do in other countries, and they imitate us as well. In this country, we are now in the process of copying some of the worst mistakes ever made in Europe. I think we are capable of more. I think we are capable of doing some original thinking in Canada—to lead the show and let the others copy us—to have the best mousetraps. I would like you to read the Report of the Federal Task Force on Housing and Urban Development. It is still, after visiting a number of countries this summer and reading their latest information, the most progressive document on the subject that I have yet seen. So take a look at it. But examine it critically and then make up your mind that the job can be done.

In considering the complexity of urban life and the problems we must solve, we cannot avoid asking the questions: Aren't they beyond us? Isn't it too great a problem for us to solve? The answer, I suppose, is: If we don't take it seriously enough—yes. If we take it seriously enough, we can do it. If we could apply to this range of problems the kind of complex management that was used in solving the anti-ballistic missile system, for example, we could do it. The Apollo-type management, where the best brains of a nation are harnessed, could be invoked to solve this whole range of interconnected problems. If we do, I am convinced that we can build new cities and rebuild existing cities, so that people can put down their roots and have signposts that mean something to them. At the same time, we could have a transportation system that would place within easy access the arts, the great centres of commerce, industry, and the excitement of great city life.

I know in my heart that the problems of housing and of cities are solvable. This is one area in which we should and could pioneer. Many of the skills that we would develop are exportable skills and we could use them to our advantage, not just in Canada, but around the world. I hope that the Liberal Party will be the vehicle for this. It has been a party of reform ever since I have been around. That is the reason I joined it and that is the reason I am still a firm supporter of it.

11

A Comment
Edwin Pivnick

The problems of the metropolitan area are unprecedented in our history. The metropolis of Toronto is 240 square miles in area and today contains 30 percent of the people in Ontario. Despite this, the cabinet portfolios which are most concerned with the metropolis have gone in the past to ministers from smaller centres. While in theory a member of the provincial house is responsible to the whole province, in fact he is influenced greatly by the views expressed at home and, in caucus, from similar ridings. Over the years these have been largely non-urban views, and the Ontario practice has been, and often continues to be, to view Metropolitan Toronto with suspicion and resentment. In the past, no united persuasive voice has been speaking to the Cabinet with feeling and understanding of the urgent problems and needs of the metropolis. The legislative changes which must be made are required to serve special needs, not special privilege. Politicians must not continue to be governed by past attitudes of staking out areas of power—but rather must divide powers and responsibilities so that the dominant consideration is the most efficient way to serve the needs of the people. Of course, this requires agreement on constitutional matters and rational taxing statutes and divisions of revenues; nevertheless it is not enough to talk of virtuous ends that can only be reached in the future when these changes are made. There are many important reforms which can be made now.

Some suggestions:

1. There should be a permanent standing committee composed of designated members of the Cabinet, the Metropolitan Toronto Council Executive Committee and designated members of the Metropolitan Toronto School Board. This committee should meet at least three or four times a year to discuss problems of the metropolis and should have a permanent secretariat composed of the deputy minis-

ters of the portfolios that are most involved with urban problems, and their counterpart commissioners in the metropolitan government. Other provinces sit down regularly with our provincial representatives (as in my view they should), usually hundreds of miles away, to discuss problems of mutual concern, while the representatives of Metro Toronto, as such, representing two million people and distant a two-stop subway ride, do not. In direct face-to-face exchanges, problems of the metropolis can be catalogued and provided for in an atmosphere of planned preparation rather than dealt with on an ad hoc basis, as often is done presently when a municipal financial crisis is imminent.

2. The requirement that the Ontario Municipal Board approve the capital expenditures of the Metropolitan Toronto government and its area municipalities should be rescinded. For Metro this approval can be given by the new committee suggested above. The provincial financial guarantees should be behind major important public projects now beyond the scope of the municipality to initiate within the confines of the present methods of approving capital works programs. If we do this, the Toronto waterfront could be immediately reclaimed for the public use of all Ontario residents.

3. The present provincial grants to the Metropolitan Toronto government and its area municipalities (and the rest of the province) should be abolished. These grants, are based on outdated philosophies. They should be replaced entirely by grants in aid and/or unconditional grants. Most of the present grants depend on the municipality first providing for or making an expenditure and the province then contributing part of the cost. Accordingly, the best fiscal responsibility in these areas will not result at the municipal level when it is known that for every dollar spent the province will contribute a whole or a part of another dollar. This also brings the province into areas where it should not be concerned in checking out and approving programs, and inefficiency and duplication result. An unconditional grant based on population, residential assessment or another criterion makes a sum available to the municipal government which should be wholly responsible for its allocation and distribution among competing municipal requirements, with priorities established by the municipal government.

4. Immediate initiatives should be taken to pool industrial assess-

ments and taxes in designated areas and to distribute this tax revenue equitably among participating municipalities. No elaboration is required to imagine the dramatic effect this could have on improved planning and decreased industrial land prices in the designated areas.

5. We must make a greater effort in confronting pollution of all kinds: water, air, noise, signs and the whole environment. Some years ago when Hydro considered it important to change from 25 cycle to 60 cycle, a very expensive and pervasive program was undertaken in Metropolitan Toronto. Every home, every business, every building was visited, and the change was made. Are we prepared to pay this price to fight pollution? If coal or oil-burning furnaces, for example, were identified as causes of pollution, would we be prepared to pay the price to change these over and prohibit them in the future? Are we prepared to ban the internal combustion engine in Metro unless it can be made pollution proof? Are we prepared to give the Ontario Water Resources Commission the authority to go into an offending industrial premise and close it down? Should Hydro Commissions continue to operate as independant authorities, or should they now become departments of Municipal Councils, at least in the large urban centres, so that electrical rates may be struck as part of the overall municipal budgeting which might also provide for the orderly, staged and continuous burial of hydro wires? What controls or limitations should be placed on the sign and billboard industries? If confiscatory controls are enacted, are we prepared to pay compensation in the same way this is done when real property is expropriated? Jobs, and accordingly the well-being of people, depend on the answers that are given to these questions. It is not enough to say that we are anti-pollutionists; we can all agree on that designation. What we have to decide now are the proper priorities and programs to take into account, the financial and other problems connected with the goal that we wish to reach, and to get on with the job.

6. Highways 400 and 401 have revolutionized the travelling and recreational habits of the residents of Ontario. The metropolis is a mecca to which all are drawn at one time or another, and planning and transportation studies must recognize this. We need at once a provincial plan which will publicly identify proposed future growth centres and which by implication will give direction to policies and budgeting of public agencies such as conservation authorities, the

Ontario Water Resources Commission, the Department of Lands and Forests, and others.

7. It is necessary to remember constantly that the courts exist to serve the people—not the judiciary, not the legal profession, not any other group: All appointments, all procedures, all administration must be made and understood in this context. Bail, night courts, all-year sittings, fixed trial dates and dozens of other reforms are urgently required to make the rule of law and administration of justice relevant, modern and acceptable to our people.

8. It is submitted that the Metro Council alone should have the power to appoint the members of the Metro Police Commission and that judges should not be eligible for appointment to police commissions generally. Judges should be in the courtroom, where they are needed to discharge their important judicial duties. The semblance of connection between judiciary and police, which is contrary to our traditional separation of powers, should be ended. The test should be how this appears to the mind of the man in the street, not to the more sophisticated person used to making such distinctions.

9. It has long been recognized in Ontario that many municipal building codes perpetuate waste and the use of yesterday's materials and methods. The provisions often conflict from municipality to municipality. For years an effort has been made to have a uniform national building code, but as the years pass the diversity continues. An Ontario building code, applicable to all municipalities of Ontario and provincial agencies, can be enacted at once, based on what is expected to be contained in the National Building Code, to which it can be made to conform later. Code uniformity will help Ontario make use of new technology, as architects and engineers are presently inhibited from developing cost-cutting innovations.

To advance and reform municipal government in Ontario has been a difficult, inch-by-inch process. Most meaningful changes that are required must be authorized by the Provincial Legislature. The municipality is otherwise powerless. The present attitudes about the metropolis that prevail at Queen's Park are outdated and must be changed. The Cabinet and Provincial Legislature must not see itself in competition with Metropolitan Toronto, nor must the rest of Ontario continue to be suspicious and resentful of the metropolis in the belief that this is an area favoured by the provincial government to the detriment of the rest of the province; it is equally inappropriate for the resident of the metropolis to fail to understand the legitimate problems of those not resident in the large urban areas. The cities require the money and authority for the jobs they must do; that authority and influence should increase rather than be eroded. The rate of change in this technological age is so fast that the fabric of a city can be altered beyond redemption in a short period. As an indication of this nearby, compare the style of life and municipal condition between the city of Buffalo and the city of Toronto twenty years ago and today. As the welfare of the metropolis of Toronto goes, so goes the welfare of the whole province because the metropolis is the fulcrum to which the economic and other welfare of the remainder of the province is inescapably tied. There has been a failure of our political leaders to show a sense of urgency in these overpowering and perilous times. I hope we shall have the vision and the courage to meet the challenges before us.

12

Regional Government in Southern Ontario
Dennis Hefferon

A dominant characteristic of industrial societies is the concentration of masses of people in relatively few urban centres.* The Economic Council of Canada has pointed out that Canada is no exception. In fact, the rate of urban population growth in Canada exceeds that of any other advanced western industrial society *including* Great Britain and the United States.

The growth of population in the study area of the Metropolitan Toronto and Region Transportation Study strikingly illustrates the point. The area (or "region") is centred on Toronto, extends north to Barrie, west to Guelph and one hundred miles along Lake Ontario from Hamilton to Bowmanville. It comprises about 3,200 square miles. In 1951, its population was 1,695,000 and in 1964, 2,800,000. It is projected to be about 4,000,000 in 1980 and about 6,400,000 thirty-one years from now at the turn of the century. The economic, social and governmental problems generated by growth of this magnitude and the increasing concentration of people in a few centres are tremendous.

While the problems of the Metropolitan Toronto and Region Transportation Study area differ in degree from those of other major urban centres in Ontario, they do not differ in kind. Their solution will have a decisive impact on the conditions under which people now live and the way generations yet to be born will live. This unprecedented growth has provided Ontario with a challenge and an opportunity to shape a human environment for our people.

How has Ontario responded to this opportunity and challenge? In *Design for Development, Phase II*, the Prime Minister stated

---

* This paper is concerned only with the part of Ontario organized for municipal purposes in which, of course, most of the province's population and employment opportunities are concentrated. Nonetheless, it is staggering to note that only about 10 percent of the Ontario area is organized for municipal purposes. See, *Government Reform in Ontario*, a report of the Ontario Economic Council, p. 21. (Toronto, 1969.)

that the Government "accepts the responsibility for guiding, encouraging and assisting the orderly and rational development of the province", while at the same time indicating that "the efforts of the Government should be complementary to the private sector of the economy in helping to create an atmosphere for growth and development".

To judge by actions and not words, however, the Government's responses to date have been tentative and piecemeal.

Economic and physical planning continue to be treated as diverse instruments rather than as tools to be used in tandem in handling a common set of problems.

The motive power for physical planning continues to reside in the municipalities while the responsibility for economic planning is that of the Department of Economics and Development (and the regional economic councils acting under its aegis) and Treasury. The location of industry in development areas has been encouraged through low-interest loans, but a comprehensive economic plan has not been adopted; economic growth points have not been selected, nor have effective techniques for securing the growth of these points been fashioned.

Further, and most importantly, Ontario has yet to reach the point of taking conscious decisions as to the appropriate direction of urban growth and the strategic deployment of people and employment opportunities apart from providing some incentives to encourage the location of industry in selected development areas. The failure to take conscious decisions on these matters and to fashion appropriate institutions and techniques to attain the objectives does not mean that decisions are not taken. In this area, as in others of life, the failure to take a conscious decision is in itself a decision of great importance.

Urban centres have been allowed to expand in a largely formless pattern and to coalesce with other centres. No limitations have been placed either on their ultimate spatial extent or population. The opportunity of linking the city with the countryside has not been taken. Balanced centres of growth can hardly be described as even a gleam in the Government's eye despite their advantages as places to live. This is, of course, in sharp contrast to England, where the decisions to contain urban sprawl through the establishment of green belts and to disperse population into balanced communities (new towns) were taken more than two decades ago.

On the other hand, the Government has embarked on a program to reform the structure of municipal government by creating urban-centred regional units of government. A number of local government reviews have been established to consider structural reforms in specific municipalities or counties, statements of Government policy have been issued and legislation has been enacted for the Ottawa-Carleton, Lakehead (Thunder Bay) and Niagara areas.

Some of the reasons why structural reform is crucial to the solution of problems resulting from urbanization, and to the very survival of local government itself, were detailed in the report of the Smith Committee, the Beckett Committee and the Select Committee on Taxation.

The 935 first tier municipalities existing in 1966 with a median population of 1,775 simply cannot cope with the problem of providing personal and environmental services and shaping the patterns of urban growth in the 1970s and beyond.

The choices seem to be either reform or continued erosion of local government functions by their assumption by the central government. It is important to note that the three years or so preceding *Design for Development, Phase II* saw the assumption by the Ontario Housing Corporation of a dominant role in the provision and administration of public housing, and the Ontario Water Resources Commission's entry into the business of providing primary sewerage and water services on a metered basis to municipalities within Peel County. This opened up, as a practical matter, a large part of the country for development in the near future.

In *Design for Development, Phase II*, the Government chose the path of structural reform. However, it is clearly not its intention to establish a new structure of local government throughout Ontario at a single point of time. Reform is to take place piecemeal on the basis of "priority of need", despite the recommendations of the Smith Committee to the contrary.

This is a vital point because without comprehensive reform of the entire structure it is difficult to see how economic and physical planning can be linked and how the critical strategical decisions outlined above can be taken and implemented.

What criteria are to be used by the Government in designing the new regions and how are they to be organized internally?

The criteria adopted by the government were listed by the Minister of Municipal Affairs in the Reply to the Speech from the Throne in December, 1968.

(1) First and foremost, the region should be urban-centred and so should exhibit a sense of community identity based on sociological characteristics, economics, geography and history, while at the same time they should be large enough so that local responsibilities can be performed efficiently by taking advantage of economies of scale.

(2) Ordinarily, the minimum population of a region should be 150,000 to 200,000.

(3) The region should be urban-centred in the sense that it will cover the major urban centres and the surrounding areas which together share social, economic and physical services. Urban and rural areas are to be linked together.

(4) Most significantly, the new regional government boundaries should be usable by other institutions—both provincial departments and agencies and local units of education.

The decision as to whether the internal structure of a regional government should be one tier (like Metropolitan Toronto) is to be made on a case by case basis. Size of the proposed region, population distribution, distribution of fiscal resources, physical and social geography and local attitudes are the relevant factors to be considered in reaching a decision on this question.

The distribution of powers between two-tier units, in general, is to follow the recommendations of the Smith Committee. For example, capital borrowing would be a regional responsibility, while there is to be a division of responsibility for the preparation and implementation of planning policy within the region.

What decisions or actions have accompanied the words? The picture is, on the whole, quite disappointing.

A one-tier or unitary system of local government has been established in the Lakehead over an area which includes enough land to accommodate urban growth over the reasonably foreseeable future. The responsibility for planning has been reposed in this radically strengthened government. The structure of power and resources of this new regional government are such as to make the management of urban growth in the region a realistic possibility.

Two-tier regional governments have been established in Ottawa-Carleton and Niagara; again the hallmark is the linking together of town and country.

In the dominant region of the province—roughly that covered by the Metropolitan Toronto and Region Transportation Study area—the picture is simply not promising. What is called for is a structure of government that will enable questions of regional significance to be decided and decisions implemented by one regional government.

Instead, the Government is moving towards the establishment of three distinct so-called regional governments including Metropolitan Toronto—in all five or six regional governments in what is a single socio-geographic region. Further, the Metropolitan Toronto Planning Area is to be reduced from 720 square miles to 240 square miles to correspond with the area of the Municipality of Metropolitan Toronto. Fragmentation of planning rather than being reduced or eliminated, evidently is to be increased as a result of deliberate Government action.

From a planning and functional standpoint this movement is nonsense. It is understandable only in rather crude political terms—the containment of the power of Metropolitan Toronto Council in relation to that of the province. Indeed, the Minister of Municipal Affairs was reported to have stated frankly that it is "vitally important to form a strong regional area to sit between Toronto and Hamilton". Why? one may ask. The creation of such a structure will not encourage the physical containment of either Hamilton or Toronto—indeed, the very reverse is likely to be true.

Coordination of planning within the Metropolitan Toronto and Region Transportation Study area evidently is to be left to cooperation between the regional governments in the vital planning area, even though the joint planning board vehicle to foster inter-municipal cooperation has not had a successful history in Ontario.

For myself, I cannot help but agree with the most renowned city planner in Canada, Mr. Hans Blumenfeld, who observed:

It would be ironic indeed if the smallest and least developed regions of Ontario were empowered to control their own development but the province's largest and most mature region would be under the tutelage of Queen's Park!

The emerging picture in other areas rather tends to indicate that

88

the Government will delineate regions on the basis of existing county boundaries rather than on the basis of socio-geographic and economic criteria. In this, as in other areas, the dead hand of the past is to rule the future.

For example, a separate local government review has been constituted in Norfolk-Haldimand, prompted by the proposed establishment of new steel plants. Yet, functionally, this area, when the plants are operational, will be linked to Hamilton-Wentworth.

In summary, then, it is clear that the opportunity presented to fashion a new revitalized structure for local government is not being seized to the full and, in fact, decisions that can only be described as retrogressive are being taken in the vital Metropolitan Toronto and Region Transportation Study area.

What should be done?

First. Strategic decisions should be taken dealing with the optimum deployment of people and employment opportunities throughout the province. Questions such as the desirability of containing the physical growth of urban centres by the creation of green belts, the desirability of dispersing population and employment opportunities and the legal techniques to accomplish this should be faced up to. Part and parcel of the regional government problem in Ontario is the development of a regional strategy at the central level.

Second. Outside the area roughly covered by the Metropolitan Toronto and Region Transportation Study area, strong regional governments should be established. The minimum population target of the Government—150,000 to 200,000—is acceptable, but the boundaries of the urban regions should be determined on the basis of geographic, economic, and sociological considerations. These regions should be large enough to accommodate about twenty years growth and to this extent should link the city and the country. However, rural areas outside urban regions so defined should not be included within the area of jurisdiction of the regional government merely to ultimately produce a map of southern Ontario which shows the entire land area with one or two exceptions within a regional government. Minimum standards for personal and environmental services in rural areas outside regional governments can be met through the adoption of a technique suggested by the Smith Committee, contracts with neighbouring urban regional governments for the supply of the services, the rural government receiving fiscal support from the province. If one of the aims of reform is to strengthen local government by uniting those whose community of interest is urban, it makes no sense and is positively undemocratic to create a political unit in which rural interests are submerged in an urban-dominated government.

Third. Whether the structure of regional government is one or two-tier, each council should be elected directly on a representation by population basis. It is naive to expect that local councillors will think in regional terms on the days when the regional council meets, but not otherwise.

Fourth. The "priority of need" concept for determining the timing of the restructuring of local government should be abandoned. The conditions are now ripe for comprehensive change; it is needed and the opportunity should be seized. Without comprehensive reform it is difficult to see how the strategic decisions I have described as urgent could be effectively implemented.

Fifth. Each regional government, whether or not it is single or two or more tier, should be responsible for the preparation of a comprehensive plan. Consistent with provincial strategic decisions, it should face the question of the desirable deployment of people and employment opportunities within the region. Further, the regional government should be much more actively involved in land development than local governments have been in the past. Specifically, it should have and use land assembly and development powers to implement its plans. Finally, it should be responsible both for housing and welfare, as well as for the provision of primary services such as sewerage and water.

Sixth. The internal structure of the government for each region, whether two-tier or one-tier, can be settled on a case by case basis. However, to strengthen participation by individuals in local government, in all cases a new unit of government is desirable. It would encompass an area within a region having a community or identity of its own, like the area covered by a voluntary community association, and would be governed by an elected community council. The council would have power to raise revenue up to a maximum fixed by the regional council and broad power to spend the money on community objects, including but not limited to recreational and cultural facilities. For reasons of economy and efficiency, the community council's tax impost would be collected by the regional government. The establishment of a community council would not be mandatory;

rather it would depend on local initiative on application to the regional government. The regional council would be given broad power to define the territorial jurisdiction of each community council and power (analogous to that of the Ontario Labour Relations Board), in effect, to certify a community association to constitute it a unit of government.

Seventh. Metropolitan Toronto and Region Transportation Study area should be considered as a single region for governmental purposes, subject to the exclusion of parts clearly outside urban growth requirements for the next twenty years.

Eighth. A single tier regional government for the entire Metropolitan Toronto and Region Transportation Study area would be too large to allow meaningful local participation in it or access to it. A two-tier structure should be adopted, supplemented by the community councils, if locally desired. The second tier units should be large (encompassing, if you like, sub-regions) with populations in the range of 200,000 to 1,000,000. They would be large enough to provide the resources and conditions to attract top drawer staff and would have geographic areas of responsibility large enough to allow services to be provided efficiently and effectively. The allocation of specific responsibilities between the two tiers could follow that recommended by the Smith Committee.

13

Planning Politics and People
W. E. Thomson

The interrelationship of people, planning, and politicians is a vital aspect of modern urban living. Few other functions of a modern city reach as deeply into a person's life, from childhood to old age, as planning does. Parks and schools, streets and walkways, recreation facilities and places of employment, major arterial locations and transit ways, urban renewal and housing, even cemetery locations—all are within the planner's realm. To cope with these, the planner has several tools at his disposal—zoning, redevelopment, rehabilitation, subdivision control, master plans, capital budgets, staging of development and public relations. If he is not involved in maintaining relationships between each function and each age and income group, then he is not a planner. The involvement is with people, and where there are people, there is politics. People, politics and planning cannot be separated.

The history of planning in Ontario has not always been a happy one. This has been due largely to the separation of the professional planner from the council. Planning is a relatively young discipline in Ontario. Before 1950 the city engineer fulfilled the planning role in most municipalities across the province. Moreover, these same engineers were the prime consultants in the private field. In the quickly developing countries, however, engineers soon found that they could not cope with everyday physical problems and at the same time worry about zoning, subdivision design and long-range planning. To bridge this gap, the Community Planning Branch was formed in the 1950s to organize planning boards. A few of these early boards made significant contributions to their communities, but the majority did not, existing to this day in name only.

As the individual communities expanded the boards were unable to keep pace with the demands for information and advice from their respective councils. Clearly, professional assistance was needed. Some municipalities allowed their boards to retain planning consultants. This approach is adequate for municipalities with a moderate growth rate; there is time to wait for studies, to arrange retainers and to draw up budgets. Faster growing communities, however, found that their original planning concepts were out of date almost as they were conceived. Councils, faced with ever more expensive revisions and by-law changes, often felt their planning boards had let them down; board-council relations became distinctly cool in some areas.

Municipalities in the 25,000–30,000 population range began to hire permanent planners, whom they placed, unwisely I believe, under the jurisdiction of the planning boards. By making planners employees of the boards rather than of the city, the municipalities contributed to the already widening gulf between politicians and planners.

As the problems grew, the Community Planning Branch encouraged communities to band together to form joint planning boards. These have been a mixed blessing. True, better funding for planning appeared. In most cases, the largest municipality in each area had the biggest development problems; but recommendations from its board and staff were subject to review by the area board and staff. Council resented the "interference" of the area board. The smaller communities in the planning area, on the other hand, felt threatened by the central municipality. Area planning boards deteriorated in many cases into arenas where the two lower tiers of planners became rivals, to the detriment of the whole area. As the controversy raged, the planners withdrew even further from the politicians. "Planning and politics don't mix" became a common cliché of the 1950s, even in the Community Planning Branch. Relations began to improve by the late 1950s and early 1960s. Some cities started employing planners directly. Instead of making them accountable to the boards as had been done previously, they loaned them to the boards as chief consultants. In this way, the planner could be closer to the people, for, as an employee of the city, he would be responsible directly to the elected representatives of the people—the aldermen—rather than to an appointed planning board.

But we are now moving towards regional forms of government and larger planning area jurisdictions. Can we adjust again to these circumstances to ensure continued good relations between politician and planner? The example of my own city may provide some answers.

As Planning Director of Kitchener (population 100,000 plus), I am a department head and directly responsible to Council. I am also the prime consultant to the planning board and its secretary-treasurer.

In my capacity as planning director, I attend every meeting of Council and its Committee of the Whole to advise and answer questions as needed. I also attend every meeting of the planning board and its Committee of the Whole as planner and secretary. Through me, all the board's opinions go to Council, and all those of Council go to the board. My own opinions go first-hand to both groups. Because of the pivotal position of the planner in Kitchener, the final planning report and recommendations that go to the board are identical with those that Council receives. Liaison has never been a problem.

We have gone one step further, however, in Kitchener. By special legislation, the province gave the City of Kitchener the coordinator-coordinating committee type of government administration. The coordinator (not unlike a city manager) is chairman of the coordinating committee, which is composed of the mayor, the city engineer, treasurer and planner. Because the planner is part of the executive team of Council, his relationship to Council and the people could not be closer.

As a member of the administration team of my city, I am automatically a member of every major committee, such as budget, capital, forecast, industrial land sales, civic centre, and so on. This background knowledge is indispensable to my planning function.

The Kitchener situation can easily be adapted to the new regional governments being introduced in Ontario. Unfortunately, in the two-tier systems already under way, a two-tier system for planning has been proposed, whereas financing, police and fire control are to be one-tier systems. It is a mistake, I feel, to separate planning into a two-tier staff system. Liaison between politicians and planners is much easier to maintain if the function of planning is not split. Confusion over jurisdiction, conflict of personalities, differences of opinion, and frustration among various political levels as well as among planners can all be avoided with a one-tier system for the planning function.

The long-range planning and research functions, as well as the administration and major policy forming functions, should remain at the central metro offices. To ensure harmony between the lower tier (borough councils) and the planners, a deputy planner with the

94

necessary staff for carrying out local planning functions should be established in each borough. This type of administration of planning will ensure the carrying out of one master plan, one set of policies, one set of standards, with only minor variations at the borough level, if necessary. Staff meetings once a week between the director and his deputies will keep channels open and ideas flowing. If the director is placed on the major metro administration team, coordination is assured.

Planning and politics must be interwoven so that they work in concert for the benefit of the people. Only when planning is a one-tier function, regardless of the governmental structure, and only when the planner is part of the administrative team, will the interrelationship of people, planning and politics grow strong and benefit all three. Politics, people, planning. People, planning, politics. The order doesn't matter, when they become one.

14

Convulsions in the Agricultural Industry
John Phillips

It is not easy to predict what will happen in Canadian agriculture over the next fifteen, let alone twenty-five or thirty years. To say that we live in an era of rapid change has become a cliché, but it is nonetheless true; particularly true when discussing agriculture. While the industrial revolution transformed the manufacturing industry more than a century ago, agriculture still has to complete its metamorphosis.

True, the tractor, fertilizers and chemicals have wrought a major change in agricultural technique, nonetheless they should be likened to the larval stage in development. The pupa stage is just around the corner. In fact it has already arrived in the laboratories, experimental farms and on the farms of the most advanced innovators. This is the genetic and nutritional revolution which will do more to change the substance and structure of agriculture than perhaps anything else. And when revolutions have passed, we will see the complete disappearance of what has hitherto been considered a tranquil and idyllic way of life; but a way of life that has been unrewarding financially to many farmers in this country.

A sampling of this genetic revolution can be seen in the chicken broiler business. Twenty-five years ago more than 100,000 Ontario farmers boasted of chicken flocks. One could drive into any barnyard and see a few hens scratching around. A dozen hens was considered the optimum number; many farms boasted of thirty or forty, while a two hundred bird flock was thought to be really large. And when the birds had finished laying, they ended up in the roasting pot. This pattern was the same in Alabama, Guelph, Hampshire, or Westphalia in Germany. The scratching and cackling hen was symbolic of pastoral society; it proclaimed a certain way of life. And to many, this way of life was almost inviolate.

But the forces of genetics and nutrition combined to change this. The so-called "genetic nick" produced a bird that would grow rapidly under ideal conditions and convert scientifically prepared feedstuffs to white meat at an incredible conversion rate. Not so long ago it may have taken five to ten pounds of feed to produce one pound of meat. Today this conversion rate has been slashed to just over two pounds of feed to get one pound of meat. It is the same story for those birds laying eggs. Note that at this point our chickens have already reached the degree of specialization where you aim for two different types of end product.

And look at what has happened to production. Broiler chickens are now kept on highly specialized farms. Thanks to advances in medical science and the virtual elimination of age-old chicken diseases, these birds are kept in large rearing units—sometimes known as factories. Twenty and thirty *thousand* birds per farm is quite normal. In fact, anyone with less than ten thousand birds is probably looking at an uneconomic operation if he is specialized. And at least one Toronto chain store now refuses to take eggs from farms with less than five thousand laying birds. It contends that the handling costs are too high to warrant feeding these eggs into the total system.

How has this affected the farmer and the consumer? Well, the number of broiler chicken farms in Ontario hovers in the region of 750, while egg producers number around 3,500, according to latest estimates. But over the next five years this figure could be reduced to about the same level as broiler chicken raisers. Incidentally, the genetic-nutrition revolution has spilled over into turkeys. The old gobblers of yesteryear are no longer with us; at least not in the same form. You will not find three or four in the orchard. Today there are thousands to a farm—on only 450 farms!

As for the consumer, chicken has now become the cheapest of all meats. Yet only a matter of years ago "chicken on a Sunday" was synonymous with the good life, the middle class and material success. If a family could eat chicken every Sunday, it had arrived. At least George Babbitt would have agreed that this was a symbol of affluence. As for eggs—despite the erosion of the dollar and the fantastic rise in the cost of living, eggs today cost little more than they did before the Second World War.

What have chickens and eggs got to do with agriculture in general? Well, what has happened in these fields is sure to be repeated in every other sector of agricultural production. What many have regarded as an isolated phenomenon will become commonplace. However, finding the genetic nick or key for some commodities will take considerably longer than it did for chickens. Hens lay eggs every day for a large part of the year; thus it is possible to come by a large number of breeding combinations very quickly, especially when selection is done by computer.

The same procedures will be used for everything else, except that in some cases it will take a lot longer. So in reality the chicken business is just a prototype for the rest of agriculture. We are on the brink of a *genetic* and *nutritional* revolution. In fact, in the hog industry the vanguard has already arrived. There is a number of Canadian pig companies devoting a lot of money and energy to finding the right genetic nick. Selection is a lot more difficult than with chickens: sows do not have piglets every day. But they do have eight to twelve a year. So the careful innovator can make progress with beef and dairy animals. It will take longer, that is all. However, with the help of "twinning"—a surgical transplant that will get a cow to yield twins instead of the usual single calf—the pace should be speeded.

Let us look at what has already happened with genetically selected hogs. I know of one purebred Yorkshire boar that has reached a market weight of 200 pounds in 118 days. You will get the significance of this when it is realized that on many good hog farms in this province, 185 days would be considered highly desirable. And entire litters from this herd now reach market weight in anything between 122 and 128 days.

Of equal importance is the fact that crossbred pigs in this large herd are registering a feed conversion of 2.2 pounds of feed to 1 pound of meat. This is not far short of the average for the American broiler chicken industry. Incidentally, the majority of Ontario's hog farmers have been quite happy with a feed conversion of 3.5 up to 4.5—or something around twice the figure reported for genetically selected pigs. Since feed costs are by far the largest input factor in hog production, these developments cannot be overstressed.

And there is another development which could cause convulsions in the traditional livestock industry: capsulated proteins. Currently experiments in this field seem to be confined largely to Britain and Europe, but if successful they will be seized by North Americans. Basically, the capsulated protein is designed for the ruminant animal. It takes the protein through the animal's first stomach and deposits it in the second stomach, where it will do the most good. Feed conversion ratios of 1.5 to 1 are reported for sheep; there are hopes of similar ratios for beef cattle. This development will have a major impact on steers, where the current conversion ratio on concentrate feeding is 4.5 to 1. Of course the pig, with its single stomach, is not in this picture; but as outlined earlier, a major breakthrough with swine, on a commercial basis, is almost upon us.

And there is another brand new development which, if successful, could shatter the traditional feed company—roasted soyabeans. A technique has just been completed in the U.S. which permits the feeding of home grown or locally bought soyabeans to livestock. The revolutionary roasting process removes all toxicity, until now the one barrier which has prevented farmers feeding whole soyabean.

To those who are not farmers or well acquainted with agriculture, this news about a simple process means little. However, all that need be said is that the machine, which can be installed on the farm for $4,000, will save the farmer buying concentrates from his feed company—a billion dollar industry on this continent. Instead, should he keep hogs, for example, all he need do is to buy a package of pre-mix and add it to his corn or barley and soyabeans. Will this development spell the end of the feed business as we know it?

And there are other developments that will help shape agriculture of the future. Not the least will be cheap protein made from oil products; and, of course, there are the synthetic meats comprised largely of soyabean fibre. However, they are costly to make, almost as expensive as the real product, and should a breakthrough be made in cost-slashing, there still may not be a big demand from North America's affluent society.

The main strike against artificial meat is that it is just not aesthetic: it does not trickle with blood, it does not have a bone, it does not have fat that can be trimmed. In our heart of hearts all of us know that it is not meat; even the poor fishermen and pulp cutters are highly suspicious of it. However, artificial meats have a major role to play in feeding the hungry of the world, a world that is starved of protein-rich foods, but beyond this shrinking area I think the fibres have limited use—outside vegetarian households and Ireland and Poland where meatless Fridays are still observed.

Before looking at policies and programs for agriculture in Ontario and Canada, we should look at major developments abroad. Until two years ago world food authorities were predicting that the spectre of hunger would hover over India, Pakistan and many other parts of Asia until at least the year 2000. In fact, a number of so-called experts announced with confidence that the hunger problem would probably never be solved without massive population control programs.

Then to the intense surprise of most people, except Canadian, American and British farm leaders, there was a complete about-face in 1968. FAE president Adeke Boerma told a world conference of farm leaders in Tunisia that they had better concern themselves with the future problem of huge food surpluses. He added that new developments "permit a cautious optimism about the future . . . that might not have been justified even a year ago". For a United Nations offical, this admission is almost unbelievable.

The answer to this amazing change in fortune can be found in technology. Vast areas of Asia and South America are now using genetically improved seeds and stock. In the Tanjore region of India alone, the per acre yield of rice has risen *fourfold* during the past three years. This is almost entirely due to ADT-27 seed, a hybrid Japanese and local variety. And in the Punjab, wheat production per acre has been doubled by crossing a local strain with one of the new Mexican varieties.

These are not isolated cases. The Indian government is now so confident about the outcome of the new agricultural revolution, that it has set 1971 as the year of national self-sufficiency in grain production—the year in which there will be grain for all, including livestock, plus a large reserve in the event of disaster. And Pakistan has similar targets. By 1973 this vast subcontinent of Pakistan and India hopes to be exporting grain in competition with Canada and the U.S. And these targets seem quite reasonable. After all, India's 1967-68 grain crop at 100 million tons was one-third higher than the previous year.

The significance of scientific and world developments has to be taken into account before formulating plans and programs for agriculture. Who would have thought five years ago that Canada was through as a wheat exporting nation? Only a few, and they were regarded as heretics of the worst possible type. Today many people think the unthinkable, but few will actually say it in public, or are prepared to base programs on what has to be a fact of life.

100

Our prairie granaries and elevators are bulging with surplus grain, yet there are no overseas markets in sight apart from traditional outlets such as Britain. Even if one or two major export sales appear over the next year, our federal government should still be thinking in terms of scaling down a large part of Canada's hard wheat production. Society should be thinking in terms of setting up large Manpower job retraining programs in the western provinces and paying farmers large sums of money to take these courses during the winter months. At the same time, light industry should be given incentives to locate or expand in the prairie regions.

Such an approach is far more humane than distributing periodic subsidies and advance grain payments. To hold out hope where there is none is completely dishonest. And such a program, while politically unpalatable, would nonetheless be easier for our Liberal government to pursue. After all, there are few Liberal seats between the Manitoba and B.C. borders. This may sound like the worst type of political pragmatism, but it just happens to coincide with the only reasonable, realistic approach to the grain problem.

Of course the more progressive western farmers have seen the writing on the wall. Up to eighteen months and two years ago some of them swung into livestock production as a means of marketing their grain. However, it could be asked if many of these operations will be viable in the long run. Much of the husbandry is second-rate by Ontario standards and some of the stock, particularly hogs, leaves much to be desired. The animals may consume a lot of the surplus grain, but the owners know little about growth and conversion rates.

Over the next few years the East is going to face heavy competition from the prairies; the sort of competition that does not make economic sense but nonetheless is real competition. Probably the Ontario farmer's only hope of staying ahead in this distasteful rat race is for him to make the utmost of our advanced technology. In fact, this should be Canada's approach in the world of the future.

Instead of exporting hard wheat and grains, I can see this country, basically Ontario, exporting parent stock from our genetically selected grandparent herds; we will be exporting sperm; we will be exporting know-how; we will be exporting management techniques; we will be exporting management systems. In other words, we will be exporting the fruits of our technological genius.

This is no wishful thinking. We have been shown the way by pioneers such as Donald Q. Shaver of Galt and his genetically selected chickens. It is interesting to note that Mr. Shaver has a large chunk of the British and European market and his organization now engirdles the world. What a pity he was compelled to become an offshoot of an American corporation, largely because he could not secure expansion capital in large enough quantities from Canadian sources.

Any government wishing to secure a stake in the agricultural future of this country has to make provisions for expansion and growth of this type. Unfortunately governments and their civil service arm are still too rooted on the past. They think in terms of traditional patterns, rather than in concepts for the future. Why, for example, are there ceilings of $100,000 on federal syndicates loan legislation and provincial cooperative loans? Today, this is a relatively small amount of money for the aggressive farm group expanding to meet domestic markets, let alone export demand. Early in 1969 one Ontario farm business, not strictly a cooperative (it does not have the word co-op in its name; what a delicious piece of bureaucracy), wanted $250,000 to build new storage space.

Since this company was not strictly a manufacturer, it could not get a forgiveable loan—an outright gift—accorded the rest of industry. However, it was also barred from getting a co-op loan, the government possibly would have stretched a point or two, because the $250,000 was far in excess of the legal limit. Surely it is high time governments started getting in step with the times. Needless to say, this farmer-controlled organization has opened markets in various countries, including the African continent.

All these great developments that will determine our future cannot be achieved without a high degree of coordinated research, particularly in the field of science. At present there is no coordinated government research in Canada; each provincial and federal department goes its own sweet way—and to these we must add our agricultural universities and colleges. In addition, we have a large number of private companies and producer groups engaged in varying degrees of research.

But where does all this activity lead us? The answer is self-evident. Surely the time has arrived when agricultural research has to be coordinated *effectively* by one body; a body that is well financed and armed with limited directive powers. The aim should be a mixed corporation, part private enterprise, part government, part university—but having real powers. However private enterprise, which includes marketing boards, should play the leading role. Government leadership in the research field is not impressive; if anything, it has rather a dismal record.

Spotty research or lack of any research is beginning to infuriate many farmers. There is one farmer in eastern Ontario who became tired of having his questions about barley sidetracked. Finally, two years ago he smuggled a European barley variety into this country. He multiplied it and has now achieved an illegal yield of 120 bushels per acre, almost double his previous yield with a Canadian variety. Now officials in the Canada Department of Agriculture know about this, but they are keeping silent. Possibly they are saying nothing for two reasons: first, they told this farmer that British and European barley did not do so well in this country; second, they have spent most of their Eastern Canada grain research money on corn. This could have been a great mistake, but they are not going to admit it.

So farmers are still no better off. But it is likely that many of our farmers would have greatly improved incomes if this imported barley variety could be tested under general conditions, and if successful, approved for use in this province. Agriculture must have answers to questions like this.

And these answers have to come quickly. If we are to rely on the traditional approach, there will be a long wait. Farm groups, whether hog producers, beef producers, or grain producers, should sponsor research by way of a sustained program of grants to universities. This would give farmers better returns than perhaps any other investment. For example, a ten cent checkoff on every Ontario hog would yield $300,000 a year for research. More important, farmers through their own marketing organization would be directing this research. But I would be happier if this research were part of a well coordinated program for all of agriculture. And since every program must begin somewhere, I would like to see it start in Ontario.

But coordinated research touches only a fraction of the problem facing agriculture over the rest of this century. Over the years farmers have accepted, unfortunately with equanimity, the role of being recipients of government subsidies and other welfare measures. This would not be so bad if, like most of industry, they had demanded and obtained positive government plans and programs for agriculture. Unfortunately, to quote former federal Agriculture Minister Joe Greene, they settled for one ad hoc measure after another. As a result, we still have no Canadian agricultural policy.

We can hardly blame Canada Agriculture Minister Bud Olson or Ontario Agriculture Minister Bill Stewart if they do nothing. After all, the 1969 June vote to establish a General Farm Organization to represent all of Ontario's farmers was in reality a vote in favour of the status quo—so long as it suits the farmer. And the record high beef, hog and milk prices prevailing at the time of the GFO vote plus a mountain of misrepresentation about the GFO truly buttressed the "no change brigade"

Many of the farm voters were living in an ephemeral paradise. I met a Dufferin County farmer a few days after the GFO vote. He was proud to have voted No, and as we walked along his verandah, he pointed gleefully to forty-three beef cattle mooching against the barnyard gate. To him they looked like bars of gold on four legs. At that time the price was between $36 and $38 a hundredweight in Toronto. He inveighed against marketing boards and farm organizations in general. They took too much money from him by way of checkoffs and selling fees—at least $30 a year! He was riding high and babbled deliriously about the glories of the competitive system, which I learned he had mastered well. He was oblivious to my comments about the law of supply and demand. In fact, he was going to hold his cattle for a few more days until the price hit 39 or even 40 cents a pound.

I had the good fortune to meet him again two months later. Listening to his conversation, he seemed an entirely different man. He was demanding a teeth-packed marketing board for beef cattle, complete with quotas and the power to "deal with those cattle buyers". It should be mentioned that beef prices had broken sharply shortly after our first meeting and had continued to tumble. He expounded on the wickedness of cattle buyers and the way the meat processors manipulate the market. What a painfully short memory this farmer has, and thousands like him.

But who are the farmers of Ontario? Are they the 103,000 mentioned in the DBS census figures? Or the 70,000 so-called commercial farmers, many of whom make a meagre living from agriculture? Or the 42,000 full and part-time farmers who could make a reasonable living from agriculture?

And by reasonable living, I mean those farmers who make adequate returns to resources: $2 an hour for labour, 8½ percent on investment, and between $1,000 and $2,000 a year from management. There is nothing unreasonable or outrageous about these levels. They are exceeded by many small city businesses with similar investments; and net farm returns would be greeted with scorn by most members of our industrial unions. Yet if the right type of young man is to stay in agriculture, he has to be assured that these minimum returns to resources are possible.

In Europe it is accepted that only the brightest and best young people stay in farming. The less bright and the less adventuresome head for the cities, where they can practise law or enter trade. Unfortunately we have got this order inverted in Canada, with the exception of those areas settled by the Germans and Dutch.

Ontario must develop policies specifically for those who will stay in agriculture and for those who will leave it. But what is a farmer? Is the man *grossing* $1,200 a year from a mound of rocks and starved land really a farmer? Can he really support a wife and six children? They subsist. What sort of future can this man offer his children? And of equal importance, what sort of future can society offer these children? More often than not, schooling in the area leaves much to be desired and vocational guidance is spotty. I know of numerous cases where children from this sort of farm are actually encouraged to stay at home with father. No emphasis is placed on higher education in agriculture or vocational courses. These children are being trapped into agriculture.

The question of who will or will not be farmers cannot be resolved until something is known about the shape and location of agriculture in ten to fifteen years from now. Unfortunately, little is known. For more than a decade there have been pleas for land use planning in Ontario. Nothing has happened, except studies, more studies and further studies.

How can any farmer really plan for the future—invest $50,000, $70,000 or $100,000 in land, buildings and equipment—if he is not sure he will be farming the same land in ten years from now? All he can see at the moment is a topsy-turvy, lopsided growth of the already large industrial conurbations, particularly the Golden Horseshoe. Most of this is at the expense of the rural regions.

More than likely, the politicians breathed a sigh of relief and went back to sleep again when the dean of communicators, Marshall McLuhan, said not too long ago that "the seamless electronic web of communications" will have a decentralizing force and large conurbations will become obsolete. However, there is little evidence of Mr. McLuhan's predictions proving to be accurate. In fact, if we continue to vegetate introspectively the very opposite will happen. Southern Ontario will become all Golden Horseshoe, five or six industrial enclaves of no great size, and a vast hinterland of depopulated countryside.

We need land use planning desperately. New centres of industrial growth have to be established; and with these centres must go all the appendages of the modern urban society; good high schools, highly paid teachers of top quality, colleges of Applied Arts and Technology, night schools with incentives, and greatly stepped-up Manpower training programs. It is our rural areas which can provide the people to man the new growth centres. And in creating these growth centres we will be solving the basic farm problem—too many people in agriculture sharing the same consumer.

The 1969 Farm Income Report noted that 36,000 full time farmers and 6,000 part-time farmers could supply all present markets, including those overseas. In fact, we only need this number if farmers are to get those adequate returns to resources we have talked about. But we have 100,000 "farmers"—and at the moment many of them have no alternate source of employment.

Since Canada's population continues to expand and the demand continues upwards for capital intensive food (steaks and pork chops instead of the bread, potatoes and cookies of the previous generation), I can see little likelihood of required farmers dropping below 42,000. Of course this thinking is based on the assumption that farming stays in the hands of the family—the one, two and three-man operations. It is almost impossible to overstress the need to continue the family farm. Apart from the great social advantages, it also happens to be the most efficient production unit. I have yet to see any evidence that the corporation farm is more efficient; if anything, the evidence points in the other direction.

Not until we have land use plans can the farm problem be solved. Land use planning will *not* force farmers from their farms. What it does is to give them the opportunity to plan for the future: they can make an informed decision to stay in agriculture or to phase out by degrees. One would hope that with Land Use planning, there will be growth.

What of those staying in agriculture? Since it becomes more and more technical with the passing of each year, a diploma in agriculture will be essential for new entrants by 1980. Moreover, governments may quite justly require farmers to have a diploma or show proven management ability before the recipient gets subsidies, capital grants or other forms of government assistance. Too often in the past subsidy money has been paid to all, regardless of the ability to use it. This contention may raise a number of eyebrows, but is the basic premise here any different from needed selectivity in the distribution of the baby bonus?

Unfortunately subsidies have been used as camouflaged welfare payments. They have not met the needs of the commercial farmer and have rarely been enough to aid the subsistance-level farmer. Policy makers must make a distinction between the commercial farmer who is viable or who can be made viable and the man eking out an existence. To be blunt, the latter should come within the area of welfare and retraining—not agriculture.

Those staying in agriculture have a right to know if they will be farming the same land in 1980 or 1990. But since there is no land use program in Ontario, they are in a state of confusion. Do they invest in a $30,000 hog barn now, knowing possibly the land could be sold to a developer or may be expropriated in a few years? Farmers need land use plans. These would indicate what land in a specific area would be used for. Because of the highly industrialized sprawl in southwest Ontario, land prices there are exorbitant—exorbitant for farmers, exorbitant for residential users. For some farmers the only alternative is for them to move to areas where all the disadvantages of distance from markets operate to their disadvantage.

Yet often good farming land near cities remains stagnant and dormant, awaiting the deft touch of the land developer. Developers have no concern for the good of society. Their business is to develop, and the fact that this developing could be done in a more beneficial manner is not their concern. They take the most economic course for them—and it would be naive to expect otherwise.

The result of this is that industrial and commercial development takes place in the middle of productive farm land. Often these activities result in pollution of surrounding areas. Regional land use would correct all this by designating certain areas for industry, commerce and urban housing and other areas for farming.

The effect of land use plans on farming would be much greater stability. When land is designated for farming, the owner would know that long-term investment in the farm is sound. And of equal importance is the fact that regional planning would permit the widespread use of effective land rental programs.

At present many farmers live poor and die rich, with only the tax collector benefiting. This situation is largely brought about by the farmer's lifelong scramble to buy land; every penny he makes goes into more and more land acquisition; after all, the experts have told him to get bigger and bigger.

The obvious solution to this should be for the farmer to own a basic unit and then rent additional land. But because of the uncertainty in the land market, farmland is almost impossible to rent for practically any period of time. A five-year lease is as rare as water in the Sahara desert. Yet this period of time is needed if a farmer is to plan ahead.

And what if the good farmer makes improvements to land? What mechanism is around to reimburse him? Farmers need land rental legislation—legislation that would protect both the farmer and the landowner. It should call for a standardized land rental agreement, specifying the responsibility and payments for land improvement and renovations to buildings.

Farmers located near the urban fringe are also in trouble. In recent years land taxes have soared. There is the York County farmer facing a tax bill of $5,800 on his 250 acre farm. That is greater than his total net income. Surely it would be easy to devise a mechanism to defer this type of punitive taxation until he sells the farm, and then deduct the extra taxes plus interest from the sale price of the farm. Oh, no! Our bureaucracy does not function in this manner. Is there no humanity left in government?

We have taken a look at the government's role in agriculture. But to be frank, this role will diminish. Since farmers are a rapidly diminishing segment of Canada's total population, the old days of indiscriminate subsidies according to the political climate are past. And a good thing, too.

As a substitute there should be judicious help and guidance from

108

government departments—expanded product research, market development and so on. Subsidies will still be needed; but they should be given with caution and with discrimination, perhaps employing the same criteria as are used when giving industry subsidies or tariff protection. Subsidies must have definite ends in mind, otherwise they become but a millstone around the taxpayer's neck.

And whether he likes it or not, the farmer must become increasingly self-reliant. He must chart and determine his own future, instead of turning trustfully to the government whenever trouble looms on the horizon. Unfortunately this trust in the inherent wisdom of governments and politicians has been the downfall of farmers. Here we find the amazing paradox: farmers are supposedly the last bastion of rugged individualism, yet when in trouble they are almost the first to seek the protection and comfort of big government's smothering womb.

This self-reliance will only come about when farmers assume responsibility for their own affairs; when they are prepared to finance their own organizations; when they are prepared to put their hands deep in their own pockets. They are going to have to be responsible in the marketplace; marketing their products in the volume and quality demanded by the consumer.

Until now, many farmers have produced irrespective of demand and then dumped their wares on the market with a shrug. They almost say, "How much will you give me?" They are going to have to adopt some form of supply management. If they don't, then the processors and corporations will do it for them, to the detriment of a free and healthy agriculture.

Farmers are not going to win the respect of the public, their families and their friends until they quit squabbling among themselves; until they can speak with a single voice; until they can back up some of their claims with well-researched documentation; until . . . but this calls for one farm organization that will speak and act responsibly on behalf of all our farmers!

15

Agricultural Supply Management
Gordon Hill

The main problem confronting agriculture in the coming years will be to find profitable markets for produce of the land. Agriculture should be interpreted to include farmers, the businesses supplying them with inputs and the businesses involved in moving produce to consumers. Agriculture no longer means farmers only but includes all those businesses providing products and services required in the production, processing, and distribution of farm products. Although farmers will continue to be hardest hit by poor produce markets, unsatisfactory financial returns to farmers will also create problems for businesses that serve them.

Decisions on what to produce, where, when, and how to market require farmers to be better informed than is now possible. Accurate information on supply-demand relationships for most commodities simply are not available to farmers—until it is too late. Corn markets in recent months offer an example. In the harvest period of 1968, corn sold for $1.00 per bushel. In June of 1969 the price had increased by 50 percent to $1.50 per bushel, presumably because of supply-demand conditions. A healthy industry cannot be built on these circumstances.

Many farmers need dependable advice on managing their business. Should they or should they not incorporate? If yes, on what basis? What type of records should they keep? Who can help get these records started and supervise them at regular intervals? Where is dependable income tax service available? Farm organization could logically provide this service, but if it does not, the extension service should.

A great deal of thought and discussion should be given to land use planning, supply management and related matters. Not because these are the only important subjects for farmers, but rather because the other important subjects—credit, extension, education, production research, equipment, technology, price support, production costs, quality control, grading, crop insurance, taxes, transportation, and a host of other subjects are old hat and accepted in varying degrees in most quarters. Supply management, although practised in most businesses outside farming and in some sections of farming, is considered by many persons to be a policy not worthy of farmers' consideration. The term "supply management" *means* arranging production to satisfy demand. It is *not* intended to mean producing less than demand in order to see prices skyrocket. It *is* intended to mean preventing overproduction from causing prices to plummet. It is interesting to note that producers of those commodities which have some form of supply management for processing—fluid milk, broilers, tobacco and vegetables—generally seem to have better incomes and higher standards of living than producers of other commodities. That is not to say producers of those commodities have perfect plans or have solved all of their problems; however, they do seem to have made more progress and be on firmer footing than farmers who produce without consideration for market demand.

No stone should be left unturned in our search for markets. At the earliest possible moment we should undertake a comprehensive survey of all market possibilities both at home and abroad. This may well require new ideas and a whole new approach, but we must not overlook even the slightest potential. Export markets must receive special consideration so that opportunities are not lost because of misunderstanding or failure to understand quantities and qualities required or terms and conditions of sale. New uses for farm products, new packaging and promotional ideas must be studied so as to make utmost use of latest trends and technology.

Pricing will be extremely important. Prices must be high enough to provide adequate returns to producers; however, competition will be keen and our prices must be competitive. Should price cutting result in unsatisfactory returns, we must decide whether this is a temporary condition which we are prepared to accept in order to hold the market. If our competitors have cost factors beyond our ability to match, we must be prepared to withdraw, as there is no merit in business without hope of profit.

Even though our efforts to expand existing markets and develop new ones meet with reasonable success, we cannot expect sales to keep pace with our increasing ability to produce. Technology will develop at a faster rate in the years ahead, and with it our produc-

111

tion ability. Some Canadian provinces still subsidize the clearing of land for farming. As a larger percentage of arable land, buildings and machinery comes under control of more efficient operators, production will increase. This is happening not only in Ontario, but in all developing countries; thus the strain on markets.

There is very little prospect of receiving profitable prices for an unlimited quantity of product. We have a choice: produce to the utmost of our ability and accept whatever prices are offered by glutted markets, or produce for known markets at profitable prices.

A land use plan should be developed immediately. Land with low productive capacity, located reasonably close to heavy population centres, should be reserved for recreational purposes. Where possible, buildings, particularly dwellings, should not be located on level productive land, but in more scenic areas. Some land should be put in a long-term land bank (20-50 years) which may include reforestation. Only the most productive land should be reserved for farming.

In this computer age it should not be too difficult to determine the quantities of each product required annually for home consumption, export markets, buffer stocks and food aid to developing nations. A system of contracts between producers and their marketing organizations, and processors or retailers *can* be worked out if we put our minds to it. Producers should be licensed by their own organization which would allocate contracts in accordance with historical production and ability to produce.

The mechanics and techniques required will not be easily developed. But with the brains and technology available today they can be worked out if we decide the policy is necessary.

It is time farmers and farm policy makers adopted cures to fit the problem rather than insist that farm problems respond to cures that are popular.

16

Ontario's Bilingual Future
Keith Spicer

That genial merchant of Canadian ideas and wheat, Trade Minister Jean-Luc Pepin, probably paid bilingualism the ultimate tribute in this adman's society: he said it takes the fear out of being close. Others have tried to hasten the rush to Berlitz with earthy peasant proverbs advising that the best place to learn French is in bed—as no doubt it is. Such gimmicky appeals today seem less urgently needed than in those fast-fading years when speaking French in Toronto was taken as either a confession or a provocation. Now learning French has become, at least among those pathetic crusaders nastily termed "white liberals", an unassailable orthodoxy, a Good and Patriotic Cause.

In this happy evolution, the role of large "L" Ontario Liberals has not been good enough. I would like to suggest a more positive view of a possible bilingual future for Ontario. In devising policies for the 70s and beyond, we should, I think, consider three matters: 1) the strengths and weaknesses of existing groundwork for a bilingual Ontario; 2) the principles which ought to guide us in evaluating realistic and civilized policies of bilingualism; and 3) certain concrete measures whose long-term value is already fairly apparent.

All partisanship aside, we have to recognize that the Conservative Government of John Robarts has greatly improved the climate and machinery needed to foster a reasonable justice in Ontario for the French language.

To begin, Mr. Robarts has pursued and deepened the sound old tradition of Ontario-Quebec consultations—a tradition, as Ramsay Cook has shown, linking Mercier and Mowat, Gouin and Whitney, Taschereau and Ferguson, Duplessis and Hepburn. With, in turn, Jean Lesage, Daniel Johnson and now Jean-Jacques Bertrand, the Ontario Premier has built bridges of understanding, useful not merely for joint provincial guerrilla war against Ottawa but for constructive interprovincial cooperation of potentially vital help to French-speaking citizens of Ontario.

Of no less significance in enhancing the rights of French-speaking Canadians outside Quebec was Mr. Robarts' initiative in organizing the Confederation of Tomorrow Conference in November, 1967. With the apparent backing of both opposition parties, Mr. Robarts defended before his fellow premiers and the national TV networks his conception of a Canada in which our two linguistic communities could live in equal dignity, if not everywhere with mathematically equal advantages. Also in national terms, Mr. Robarts made a statement which I think, for its sanity and courage, may be the most important heard from any English Canadian politician of this decade: he said, in effect, that if Quebec withdrew from Confederation, that would in no way diminish his support for the language and cultural rights of French-speaking Canadians in Ontario. I know a few Quebeckers who think that sort of attitude from English Canadians is a pretty good reason for staying in Canada.

More substantially, and within the province itself, the Conservative Government has moved over the past two or three years to lay down administrative and educational foundations to secure the rights of Franco-Ontarians. Reports by task forces on French in the courts, public administration and other fields are being projected into long-term policies by a dynamic band of young civil servants in the Federal-Provincial Affairs Secretariat. Bills 140 and 141, passed just over a year ago, now underpin the rights of Franco-Ontarians to their own tax-supported public schools. Language courses and a quickly growing translation bureau are helping civil servants and at least a few MLAs to incorporate French into their duties more and more as a viable working language. And a cultural agreement signed with Quebec a few weeks ago offers hope of intensified exchanges to support both the Franco-Ontarians' will to flourish and the rising enthusiasm of English-speaking Ontarians for hopping on the B. and B. bandwagon.

All that is excellent, but we are still far from the bicultural millennium. Apart from arguing that while the Government for once is right, it is not doing what is right quickly enough, one can fairly reproach the Conservative Government with two failings in this area.

First, it has recoiled from following the Laurendeau-Dunton recommendation that Ontario declare itself officially bilingual. I understand well Mr. Robarts' reasoning that in a province supposedly still peopled by Anglo-Saxon pragmatists, one does not go about declaring things that are not in fact true. This attitude is commendable in its Puritan integrity, but I question its value as a contribution to resolving the Canadian crisis (and we still have one, even though a lot of people think they resolved that problem on June 25, 1968).

Declaring French an official language of Ontario rather than merely a tolerated and rather folkloric *lingua franca* in certain sectors, would offer the following benefits: a) it would help educate the citizens of Ontario to the historic trend now confirming our province's crucial and exemplary role in national unity; b) it would support in law the present, inevitably piecemeal, progress of bilingualism in Ontario's public administration and public institutions; and c) it would tell our countrymen in Quebec unmistakably that we intend to secure for French here the same rights English has in Quebec. Official, as opposed to tacit, recognition of French would accept the fact that to some extent our bilingual message is destined for Cartesian minds: for the man or woman of French culture, principles, unreservedly stated, convey the ultimate good intention. Concrete implementation may prove gradual, but slowness can be forgiven if one accepts the guiding idea wholeheartedly. We are here in the presence of two equally honest definitions of honesty. I think, on balance, Descartes has the edge over Robarts on grounds of both clarity and effectiveness.

My second reproach to the Conservatives applies to their failure to pull off the indispensable miracle of teaching realistic French in our schools. By realistic, I mean living, Canadian French rather than bookish, European French.

For nearly all of us here, reference to Ontario high school French will evoke a shudder, a groan, perhaps a fluent, strictly English curse. As in most parts of Canada, our schools have inflicted on generations of open-minded kids a nightmarish hodge podge of offbeat subjunctives, elegant salon vocabulary (ideal for discussing offbeat subjunctives in Loire Valley castles with dispossessed countesses) and thinly-veiled contempt for the French spoken by our native French-speaking compatriots. You know the old story: "We're teaching you Parisian French, not that ghastly Quebec patois." As though Quebeckers had to choose between Oxford and Cabbagetown English.

I know of the enormous progress made in teaching French in recent years at all three levels of schooling. There are schools in this province that make the above description seem a vicious caricature.

115

But from the results I see in kids from some of the supposedly best schools around Toronto, we are still turning the great majority of our children off French instead of tuning them into it. And turning them off French means to a large extent blocking their minds to a really spontaneous, exciting dialogue with their French-speaking compatriots. Waterloo, we are told, was won on the playing fields of Eton. Canada, if ever it is lost, will fall, I believe, in the classrooms of this nation.

From these points of departure, both favourable and unfavourable, what lights should we follow to achieve a sensible and fair program of bilingualism? In addition to the principle of official bilingualism, I think we might consider the following guidelines.

1. *Persuasion through example*. Preaching about the duty of learning French or accepting the law of an officially bilingual government seems to me a disastrous way to lead people to a bilingual future. The first and most effective "propaganda" for bilingualism is a happy and honest example. For a start, I think it a basic obligation of provincial party leaders and as many as possible of our MLA's to make a fair stab at becoming personally bilingual. Pierre Trudeau gets across the reality of official bilingualism almost every time he opens his mouth. I think it a normal and intelligent thing for his Ontario counterparts to do their best, as some of them already are, to master at least enough French to get by on either end of Question Period.

Indeed, if this party seriously expects one day to form the Government at Queen's Park, I think it vital that its leader be more than passingly bilingual. Ed Schreyer has reminded us of the impact an English Canadian Premier can have by speaking easily to Quebeckers in their own language. Ontario, if it hopes to keep some leadership in remoulding Confederation, cannot much longer afford a Premier with Ontario high school French.

2. *Give people the means to the bilingual end*. No Queen's Park regime has the moral right to impose official bilingualism unless it helps the people meet this new obligation as a freely embraced opportunity—an opportunity for personal growth and enrichment, an opportunity to participate in seeking a goal that is not only worthwhile but attainable. That means rethinking from top to bottom the teaching of French in this province with a view to making French a useful vehicle of communication with other Canadians. It means studying carefully the suggestions of the Saint Denis Report on the

Cultural Life of Franco-Ontarians with the understanding that French culture in Ontario, to survive and flourish for the benefit of both linguistic communities, will need special and imaginative support.

3. *An expanded partnership with Quebec.* Any future Ontario Government must rely, to achieve the above aims, on confident and greatly expanded exchanges with Quebec. Only Quebec can offer Ontario the relevant experience it needs in French-language education, and Quebec's help in developing a bilingual public service and court system is almost indispensable. Building on this essential Ontario-Quebec solidarity should logically start under the umbrella of the interprovincial cultural agreement. But it should move on as soon as possible to include Manitoba and New Brunswick in a multilateral *entente cordiale* to offer reciprocal help in developing French culture and education—especially in working out common standards for French-language textbooks, teacher training and diplomas.

4. *Some long-term measures.* Starting from these guidelines, a future Ontario Government might consider some of the following specific policies:

a) *an interprovincial linguistic Peace Corps*: composed of second or third year university students from Quebec and Ontario. Under reciprocal arrangements, Queen's Park would offer each year several hundred, then several thousand, $3,000 scholarships to Quebec students for study at Ontario universities. In exchange for this opportunity, the Quebec students would teach French conversation and phonetics in local Ontario high schools. Later this might be extended to include elementary schools.

b) *an interprovincial summer job exchange*: to build on the above, Queen's Park ought to work with Quebec to match several hundred summer jobs in each province with students from the other. At present there is a strong demand for such jobs on both sides, and a need for efficient, centralized coordination. This could be done through the Department of Education's Educational and Cultural Exchange Service, which has already done remarkable work in initiating exchanges with Quebec. Many such jobs could be offered in government departments themselves on a matched number basis; this would quickly widen the pool of young Ontarians able to work in both languages at Queen's Park;

c) *an autonomous French sector in the Department of Education*: fully to ensure that schools for French-speaking Ontarians reflect their felt needs, the Minister of Education would appoint a second, and co-equal, Deputy Minister in charge of French schools. This would imply an entirely distinct hierarchy for French schools, in which French would be the working language and all basic educational decisions made by Franco-Ontarians. This need in no way prevent co-operation, sharing and exchange with the English-language sector.

d) *a policy of strategic bilingualism*: Ontario will always remain a predominantly English-speaking province, and French need not be superimposed on government services where it will almost never be needed. But high priority for service in French ought to be given to all provincially supported museums and tourist sites, as well as central departmental headquarters, the Queen's Park telephone exchange and, in northern and eastern Ontario, regional offices, documentation and highway signs.

e) *a special effort to attract French-language tourists*: as bilingual facilities in museums and historic sites develop, Queen's Park could make a special appeal to French-speaking tourists in Quebec. Well-written and well-adapted brochures on Toronto and Niagara Falls, as a start, and twenty or thirty French-speaking guides for these areas would not cost a great deal, but might well, with some advertising in the Quebec press, make both Quebeckers and Ontarians more aware of the province's French heritage and new commitment to bilingualism.

Whatever a future Ontario Government does to foster bilingualism, I believe it will succeed only by demonstrating that knowing another language is both realistic for the Ontario Government and fun for individuals. This does not necessarily mean, as an exasperated wag might put it, that the only sensible kind of bilingualism would demand using English for business and French for love. At the very least, however, it would suggest that when Liberal and other politicians talk about bilingualism, they should smile—instead of blushing, praising it with faint damns, or gnashing their teeth. Bilingualism, were they to rub a little more on each morning, really could take the fear out of being close.

17

The Slaughter on the Highways of Ontario
Allen M. Linden

The bloodshed produced each year by the two and one-half million cars in Ontario resembles that of a full-scale war. Over 1,500 people die on Ontario's highways each year; over 50,000 are injured every year; the damage to property exceeds $50 million yearly. What is even more horrible is that we have come to accept as inevitable this epidemic on the roads.

We have made half-hearted attempts to reduce the accident toll. The favourite tool of safety agencies and governments is to launch expensive advertising campaigns aimed at scaring drivers into driving carefully. Gory billboard signs are placed around the province, particularly at Christmas time, to frighten us into driving safely. Besides making us shudder for a moment, recent studies have shown that the millions spent on these campaigns are largely wasted.

Stricter enforcement of our traffic laws is often sought as a solution to the problem of murder by motor. Although some beneficial effect may be derived from these methods, the accidents continue to mount. The much-publicized traffic law enforcement campaign launched by the then Governor Ribicoff of Connecticut had only a minimal effect. Our obsession with stricter enforcement is unwarranted.

And what happens to the thousands of people who are injured as a result of an automobile accident? Are they adequately compensated for their financial losses? A recent study at Osgoode Hall Law School showed that 57 percent of all the people injured did not recover one cent from the other person involved in the accident. This is so despite the fact that 98 percent of Ontario drivers are insured and where the driver is insured the injured person can claim against the Motor Vehicle Accident Claims Fund. The reason for the small percentage of recoveries is, of course, the fault system, which requires the injured person, in order to recover, to prove that he was injured as a result of the fault or negligence of the other person. This is often a difficult task. And if the person injured is a passenger in a car, he has a lesser chance of recovery. This is so because the law of Ontario deprives all passengers of their right to sue their drivers except if gross negligence is present rather than ordinary negligence. The Liberal Party has introduced legislation on several occasions to abolish this iniquitous law, but the Legislature was not allowed to vote on it. Passengers should have the same right to recover as anyone else.

Even if the victim is lucky enough to secure a few dollars from the other person, he often has to wait two years, three years and even longer to get it. And the more serious the injury, the longer the injured person must wait for his payment. Nevertheless, insurance premiums continue to increase as repair and administration costs and accident figures rise.

This sordid picture must be changed. We must stop procrastinating. Bold action is needed on several points. We must recognize that it will cost money, but hundreds of lives can be saved and injuries and the social dislocation caused by injuries can be reduced.

Focusing on the driver, we must realize that exhortation and stricter law enforcement is no panacea. A major driver education campaign must be undertaken in every high school in the province. Since virtually all of our people drive, all should learn to drive properly. Licences should not be distributed until we are sure of the driver's capacity to cope with the complex situation in which he may find himself. In Ontario today, once a licence is issued to someone it is renewed automatically despite the fact that people grow older, their eyesight fails and their driving ability degenerates. We should require retesting at least every five years to ensure the good health of the driver as well as his familiarity with new rules of the road, new signs and other such things. Psychological research must be done into the causes of accidents and methods should be devised whereby we can minimize the human factors producing collisions.

We must make our highways safer. It has been shown that well-engineered roads can cut the accident toll substantially. Limited-access roads yield a smaller rate of accidents than other highways. Better signs, lighting and non-skid road surfaces can further reduce the accident rate. We should stimulate Safety Research to develop safer highways and we should implement these findings in our road building plans. For example, we could remedy the dangerous qualities of the Don Valley Parkway that have been recently disclosed.

120

Whatever we do to make the driver more careful and the roads safer, collisions between vehicles will continue. Accepting this fact, we must reduce the number and severity of the *injuries* suffered in these inevitable accidents. Our automobiles can and must be made crashworthy. Studies at Cornell University and elsewhere have demonstrated that if seat belts had been used by everyone killed in a car crash, about one-half of the lives might have been saved. And yet Ontario does not require seat belts in all our vehicles, nor does it require them to be used. The Department of Transport has recently started to encourage their use, but only in a half-hearted way. Other studies have shown that padded dashboards, roll bars, collapsible steering wheels, recessed door handles and control knobs, hydraulic bumpers, doors that can't spring open and other safety features can reduce the bloodshed on the roads. Lately, because of new legislation in the United States, some of these safety features are being introduced into automobiles. In fact, the car manufacturers, who have not distinguished themselves over the years by their altruism, are actually placing more safety equipment into their products than Ontario law requires them to. The Highway Traffic Act requires only that a vehicle have two headlights, one rear light, turn indicators, a rearview mirror, safety glass (which is not defined) and two sets of brakes (but only one has to be able to stop the car when in motion). The manufacturers are more safety conscious than the government that regulates them—they supply two rear lights, seat belts, a side view mirror and, now, padded dashboards, collapsible steering wheels and other items, even though they are not required to do so. Let us stop permitting this unnecessary loss of life and require that all vehicles be built for safety in the event of a crash. Let us require the use of seat belts by all occupants of a vehicle. If we do, we can save several hundred lives each year in Ontario.

Despite this campaign for driver safety, road safety and crashworthy cars, there will still be thousands of people injured on the highways. We must ensure that they are looked after—that they are not wanting for medical, hospital and rehabilitation services, and that at least a subsistence income is available for them. It is now nine long years since the Select Committee on Automobile Insurance was set up to study this problem. Six long years have elapsed since their final report was filed. Legislation must be introduced to implement the recommendations of the Select Committee. In March, 1963

121

it urged the expansion of "accident insurance" or the present "medical payments coverage" so that all standard automobile policies sold in the province would include such coverage. The Motor Vehicle Accident Claims Fund would provide similar coverage for those injured by uninsured drivers or hit-and-run victims. In other words, the implementation of this recommendation would provide limited benefits for bodily injury or death to all occupants of an automobile and to any pedestrians struck by that automobile, regardless of proof of fault. Certain set amounts would be paid to the estates of persons killed and to persons dismembered or who lost the sight of one or both eyes. For example, for the death of a married male between 18 and 59 years, $5,000 would be paid plus $1,000 for each additional dependant. The death of a married female of the same age would yield $2,500 plus $1,000 for each additional dependant. Loss of two hands or feet would bring $5,000, loss of sight $5,000, loss of one hand, foot or the entire sight of one eye $2,500.

In addition to these specific sums, indemnity of up to $2,000 would be provided for reasonable expenses incurred for necessary medical, surgical, dental, ambulance and professional nursing expenses. Hospital expenses over and above the coverage of the Ontario Hospital Services Commission would also be reimbursed within the $2,000 composite limit. Funeral expenses of up to $350 for each person would be provided where necessary on top of the $2,000. Weekly benefits of $35 would be paid to an employed person when totally disabled to a limit of 104 weeks, subject to an extension for an additional 104 weeks in the case of total and permanent disability. In the case of a totally disabled housewife, $25 weekly would be paid for up to 12 weeks. In neither case would payment be made for the first seven years. Only where a motorist is driving while unlicensed, while intoxicated or while in violation of the Criminal Code would he be precluded from recovery, but if such driver is killed, his family would not be deprived of compensation. There would be no interference with the injured person's right to sue the person who was at fault for his injury, except that any benefits received under the proposed new plan would be offset against any tort recovery. The Select Committee on Automobile Insurance relied heavily on submissions made on behalf of the All-Canada Insurance Federation and of a Special Committee of the Law Society of Upper Canada. The Canadian Bar Association has recently endorsed this concept. This indicates that a substantial number of those in the insurance industry and the Bar of Ontario must favour this proposal. The cost of this coverage, that is now being written on a voluntary basis in most provinces including Ontario, is only $7. It should be made mandatory.

This plan would guarantee that all the injured would be looked after without interfering with the rights of those who are presently able to recover in the courts, although one might have preferred that the upper limits be removed, that the weekly payments be more realistic, and that they should not cease after only four years. Moreover, there should be provision for partial payments for partial disability, which is far more common than total disablement in auto accidents.

This insurance can be written by the private insurance companies because they have already in operation the machinery to implement this system swiftly and inexpensively. But we must watch carefully its administration in the first few years. We cannot abdicate to the insurers the absolute power to fix rates and to cancel policies whenever they wish. Government must be a watchdog over both the rates and the insurance policy cancellations. Where a policy is unjustly cancelled, the individual should have the right to appeal this action to the Superintendent of Insurance. Insurance companies may provide valuable service, but they should not be permitted to dictate rates nor who shall be able to secure insurance.

This then is a plan to reduce the mounting toll of life taken on the highways of Ontario. A comprehensive program of driver education, a more effective licensing system, a safe road campaign and a safety car drive must be undertaken. For those who are still unlucky enough to be injured, basic compensation regardless of fault should be assured to all. As long as the private insurers serve the people of Ontario fairly, they should be allowed to write this new coverage, but if they abuse their privileges, action may have to be taken. Much more research could be done to find ways of reducing injuries, the cost of injuries and the other costs such as repair costs. But this program is only a beginning. It is time we at least tried to stop the slaughter on our highways.

18

The Future of Ontario Lies in the North
Pat Reid

I see in the not remote distance one great nationality bound, like the shield of Achilles, by the blue rim of ocean. I see it quartered into many communities, each disposing of its internal affairs, but all bound together by free institutions, free intercourse and free commerce.

Thomas D'Arcy McGee, in a debate on Confederation, 1865, in the Legislative Assembly.

When the Fathers of the Confederation decided to form a nation in the northern part of the North American continent, the decision they made was a political one. Economic and other considerations certainly were examined, but the decision to unite the four provinces was essentially political. The Fathers of Confederation at that time were extremely far-sighted but they would be a little shocked to see that the nation we know as Canada is nothing more than a strip of communities some two hundred miles wide along the American-Canadian border.

As the Canadian nation came into being as a result of a political decision, so too must the development of the North be primarily a political decision. In any discussion of the possibilities of northern development, much is heard of the economic and geographical factors which militate against any grand scheme for developing Canada's North. We seem to have a national and provincial myopia when it comes to looking northward. If we look at the experience of Russia and the Scandinavian countries, and even Israel, we can see that economics can be forced to support political decisions. The Russians, as a result of political decision, have built cities of more than a quarter million people in the frozen North to exploit the great economic factors of their North. Scandinavian countries, too, have developed their northern resources and have many large communities there. Israel, as a result of political decision, now exists as a viable economic country. In each of these cases, economics was the tool of political decision rather than the governing factor.

What is needed first, therefore, in any development of Northern Ontario and Northern Canada is a willingness and a desire for such development. Northern development will depend upon conscious political decisions on the part of both the federal and provincial governments.

The federal government is involved because of its jurisdictions over many phases of northern development, especially in transportation, communication and foreign trade. Further, any proposed plan of northern development will be so gigantic in scope that the full resources of the federal government will be necessary to make it work. The provincial government is involved because it has jurisdiction over many other facets of northern development or shares jurisdiction with Ottawa. The provincial government, of course, has primary jurisdiction over regional development, regional government and natural resources. The cooperation of both the federal and provincial governments, therefore, is absolutely necessary for any development scheme for Northern Ontario. Perhaps the development of Northern Ontario should be only one part of an expanded and continuing program on the part of the federal government for the development of all Northern Canada, such as is envisaged in the Mid-Canada Corridor concept.

The North should and must be developed. Northern Ontario comprises over two-thirds of land mass of the province, and contains a treasure house of natural resources which is the envy of our neighbours to the south. The North is relatively free of air and water pollution. It offers a quality of life in a natural environment which cannot be found in our congested and polluted cities. One of the most pressing reasons for development of the North will be, if it is not already, to relieve the pressure of urbanization and the concomitant problems of cities in the southern regions of the province. We shall see, in the not too distant future, corporations and people looking to the North where there is space, fresh air and fresh water and where recreation and leisure time may be enjoyed to the full.

There are many difficulties associated with northern development, some economic and some political. In an economic and historical sense, the North has always been exploited. The fur traders first came to Northern Ontario primarily to hunt and trap the beaver. They were followed by the lumber barons who cut down trees

125

indiscriminately and leave nothing behind. Lumber companies were followed by the mining giants who dig holes in the ground and again leave nothing behind them.

The economic history of the North has been one of exploitation and extraction, of people and corporations moving in, exploiting the available resources and moving on, leaving nothing behind them but ghost towns and unemployed. This kind of exploitation is still going on in the North with commercial activities based on the forest industry and the giant mining companies exploiting the natural resources of Northern Ontario. There now seems to be greater acceptance of some social responsibility on the part of these companies but not enough to guarantee a stable future for the people of Northern Ontario.

This economic exploitation has been linked with political weakness. The Federal House of Commons has 265 members, 14 of whom are from Northern Ontario. The Ontario Provincial Legislature has 117 members, 11 of whom are from Northern Ontario. In terms of political strength, Northern Ontario finds itself greatly outnumbered and in a position of relative political weakness. The House of Commons and the Ontario Legislature are preoccupied with separatists, wheat and hippies, and have little or no time to give to the needs and desires of the citizens of the northern part of Ontario.

This neglect and misunderstanding translates itself into legislation, which, although necessary for Southern Ontario, is broadly applicable also all across Northern Ontario. This happens time and time again. At the same time, the problems of the North are viewed through and related to the problems of Southern Ontario, while, in fact, the problems of the North are in most cases entirely different. Northern Ontario's political weakness has resulted in the unconscionable neglect of this region, especially at the provincial level. The present government neither understands nor cares about the problems of the northern part of their province. The present government, looking at the statistics, sees that their political strength lies mainly in Southern Ontario and gives little heed to the voices of the North. As a result, there are no guidelines for northern development at the provincial level and little hope that there will be under the present government.

In an economic sense, the greatest difficulty is the lack of capital. The huge projects involved in northern development require large amounts of capital. There is also a lack of the smaller amounts of capital needed for home building, apartment building and small plant building.

Financial institutions seem to be practising an unconscious discrimination against the northern part of the province. This point was brought out at the North-East Economic Conference called by the federal member of Cochrane, Ralph Stewart, and the Honourable René Brunelle, Minister of Lands and Forests. The financial institutions in the province are loath to invest in Northern Ontario. Perhaps there are too many favourable prospects in the southern part of the province. In any case, it is exceedingly difficult for a small entrepreneur to raise the necessary capital to finance any kind of project through normal lending channels. Often a great deal of difficulty is experienced in dealing with CMHC also, whose rules and regulations certainly are not flexible enough to take into consideration the special problems of northern home and apartment building.

A related problem to the lack of capital, of course, is the interest rate. Even when capital is available, the unusually high interest rates presently being charged by the banks and other financial institutions are one of the main drawbacks to any kind of development. The present interest rates are unprecedented, and when the higher costs of living and transportation in Northern Ontario are taken into consideration, any kind of individual development is discouraged.

The lack of capital is associated also with lack of entrepreneurial talent and lack of job options and opportunities. The North, therefore, loses its greatest resource, its people, who move to the southern areas where difficulties in raising capital and finding jobs are not as severe as in the North.

The high cost of living and high cost of housing are due in large part to high transportation costs. The two five-year development reports on northeastern and northwestern Ontario cite transportation costs as *one of the main factors* in the slowness of growth in Northern Ontario. These high costs apply to goods coming into Northern Ontario for the use of the residents and for construction purposes, and also to the shipment of products from Northern Ontario to southern and foreign markets. These products, mainly metallic ores and forestry products, are moved by rail. The railroads enjoy a monopoly position and are, therefore, able to charge rates which bear very little relation to cost. There is little in the way of transporta-

127

tion alternatives, for the North lacks road, railroad facilities, and airports.

There is a concomitant problem, both in services to get people from one place to another and in actual communications media, such as television, radio and newspapers. A large part of Northern Ontario, especially Northwestern Ontario, receives television news from Manitoba. There is no one radio system linking all of Northern Ontario and giving it a sense of identity. The newspapers are generally local papers interested only in local issues and therefore very inward looking. These aspects of transportation and communication, of course, add to the feeling of isolation which Northwestern Ontarians feel, even in their own northern region, as distinct from their feeling of isolation in regard to Queen's Park and Ottawa.

A great many of the problems and difficulties associated with northern development must be worked out on a long-term basis. That working out, however, must begin immediately. There are certain things that can be done now to facilitate the development of Northern Ontario.

The Liberal Party in Ontario must actively associate itself with the desires and aspirations of Northern Ontario and acquaint the party membership with the potential of the North. By doing so, it will bring renewed interest and increased pressure on all levels of government to do something about the northern situation.

The Province of Ontario should move to set up within the Cabinet a Department of Natural Resources and Northern Development. At present, responsibility for the North is divided among a number of Cabinet positions, all pursuing their own narrow objectives within their own narrow framework. There is little, if any, coordination and cooperation and, indeed, a great deal of interdepartmental fighting and jealousy exists at the present time. Responsibility is too diffuse for any strategic plan of development to take shape. It is interesting to note that there are twelve departments which are directly involved in the tourism industry and over which the Department of Tourism itself has little or no control. Therefore, *one* Department of Natural Resources and Northern Development must be established under *one* Minister responsible to the Cabinet. Within this department Parliamentary Secretaries should be appointed to take responsibility for such areas as tourism, mines, lands and forests, fisheries, wildlife, and so on under the one Minister. This would lead to a much more rational and responsible distribution of power and a great deal more coordination and cooperation than presently exists.

For a rational development policy, regional development for Northern Ontario should be instituted as quickly as possible, with the utmost cooperation and involvement of the citizens of the area. Regional government will lead to a decentralization of government authority and bureaucracy from Queen's Park. The northern people themselves will have much more direct control over their own affairs. Regional government will lead to better coordinated planning especially in such things as land use. Specialized legislation can be passed that will apply to one region only to ensure the development of that region in line with the wishes of the residents. Conditions in the North lend themselves to the setting up of two regional governments, Northwestern Ontario and the other, Northeastern Ontario.

These two government regions could implement the one-corridor concept. Presently, we have telephone lines, hydro lines, pipeline, all separately slashing their way crisscross through the bush in the heartland of Northern Ontario. Corridor planning should be undertaken so that all these facilities would be required to be built within a narrow strip. All these utilities then would run side by side eliminating the chopping and mutilation of the natural environment.

Another task that must be undertaken immediately, preferably by a regional government, is a complete comprehensive inventory of the resources of Northern Ontario. One cannot do any planning without knowing what resources are available. At the moment various government departments are doing surveys but these are restricted to the specific areas of each department's interest.

A complete survey of transportation costs must be done for Northern Ontario. Although the government has made such studies, they have not been released. For what reason no one seems to know. Transportation must be high on the list of planning priorities. It must be done so as not to ruin the natural environment of Northern Ontario. One of the reasons Northerners live in the North is because they enjoy the environment. The Department of Highways must take a more active part in the construction of roads in the North both for transportation and communication reasons. The communication system must be assessed with perhaps the advisability of a CBC station being erected at the Lakehead.

The development of Northern Ontario is going to require huge amounts of capital. This capital should come from Canadians. It may be possible to allow foreign debt capital to take part in the development of the North, but the equity should remain in the hands of Canadians. A program should be undertaken by both the provincial and federal governments to make financial institutions aware of the opportunities in the North and of their responsibilities to the nation.

A northern resources fund or northern development fund must be set up to supply capital for projects in the North. Money from this fund should be let at a reasonable rate of interest. The funding of such a capital pool could perhaps be accomplished by taxing the resource base companies operating in Northern Ontario as follows. Any natural resource company that has made a profit of over $5 million in the last three years should be taxed in a one-shot lump sum for one year at 10 percent on its profits. This tax should last for only one year and be abolished thereafter. It would provide an initial pool of funds from which individuals and corporations could borrow capital at a reasonable rate of interest. It seems only fair and just that the natural resource industries contribute in this way to the development of the North where they have made such huge profits and, in most cases, contributed so little.

The development of Northern Ontario must involve to a maximum degree the people of the North as they are the people most directly affected. As they will also be the people most directly benefited, they should have a large say in the way the development of their particular area takes place.

There should be a special program of development for the Indian people of Northern Ontario. The federal government's policy seems to be to integrate the Indian into the mainstream of white society. The educational facilities provided for the Indians should allow them enough choice that they can live their lives as they choose. Because each Indian reserve or settlement differs considerably from its neighbour, the development of these reserves must be done on a community basis. A good start in this direction has been made by the Amik Corporation in Northwestern Ontario. Amik is a voluntary organization composed of Indian and non-Indian people for the purpose of assisting poor communities mainly of Indian origin to improve their social and economic life.

The development of the North is mainly the development of the northern people. The development of the Indian must take place first at the level of the local white and Indian community.

The development of Northern Canada and of Northern Ontario remains as a last frontier in Canadian history. Northern development could give the nation a sense of purpose and national unity which it has not had since the building of the Canadian Pacific Railway. It must be a project which involves mainly people residing in the North, but which also encompasses the entire nation.

19

Responsible Government in Ontario: Will Government be up to the Task? *
Fred Schindeler

Good policies are of little value if they are not implemented in an efficient and democratic manner. Is the governmental structure of Ontario up to the task that it is going to face in adopting new policies for the 1970s?

In this paper, I will do just three things. First, I would like to say something about what is happening to our federal structure and how this is affecting our provincial institutions. Secondly, I will illustrate how our institutions have already been adapted to meet the new situation. And, finally, I will offer my own opinion as to their suitability for the task ahead.

In the mid-nineteenth century, when the province of Ontario was being formed out of the western half of the old colony of Canada, the prevailing political philosophy in the English speaking world held that the activities of government should be limited generally to the preservation of peace or the waging of war in external affairs, the maintenance of justice and order in domestic affairs and the grudging provision of those public works that could be obtained in no other way. The advocates of this concept of the negative state were never able to restrict the functions of government to the narrow sphere prescribed in their ideal model but, as Professors Corry and Hodgetts have pointed out, "they had a profound influence on the scope of government action throughout the greater part of the nineteenth century. The negative state was not merely an academic theory; it was largely realized in the scope and character of the nineteenth century governments."

So far as the provinces of Canada were concerned there were more concrete limitations on the extent of their operations than

* The editors would like to thank the University of Toronto Press for permission to use material from Mr. Schindeler's book, *Responsible Government in Ontario*.

political philosophy: the central government had taken from them all of their "great functions", and approximately 83 percent of their former revenues. Although the advocates of legislative union had not had things completely their way, they were content that the provincial administrations were so strictly curtailed in their responsibilities and means as to be little more than glorified county councils. A number of factors have worked together to give the lie to this conception of the place of the provinces in the Canadian federation.

In the first place, certain legislative fields have simply grown in proportion to the increase in population. While this is not a sufficient explanation, it has been a significant factor in the expansion of such functions as education and public works.

A second factor in the increase in provincial responsibilities has been the tendency of judicial decisions, particularly since 1882, to favour the provincial rather than the federal jurisdiction. Whether through intentional malice towards the central government or simply because of an overemphasis on the letter as opposed to the spirit of the constitution, the Judicial Committee of the Privy Council practically reversed the intentions of Canada's founding fathers. The clause in section 91 of the British North America Act which was meant to give the central government not only the residual powers (conferred also by clause 91:29) but also a general power to legislate for the "Peace, Order and good Government of Canada", was relegated to the position of an emergency clause, while heads 13 and 16 of section 92—which gave the provinces control over "Property and Civil Rights" and "all Matters of a merely local or private nature in the Province"—became the *de facto* residual clauses of the constitution. The learned judges found it increasingly difficult to find any subject matter which did not touch upon property or civil rights or which did not resolve itself into a local problem.

This process, which began during the years of Oliver Mowat's premiership, has continued into the modern era and has resulted in the provinces acquiring most of the new powers which have accrued to government.

But the factor which has most profoundly influenced the scope of government operations in Ontario has been the gradual change in the social attitudes of the people of the province. Increased specialization in agriculture and industry, improved means of transportation and communication and the massive rural to urban population shift

133

have made men less self-sufficient than they were in 1867. Economic and social interdependence have given an impetus to government intervention, and gradually the people have come to expect the government to take a creative part in establishing a viable economy and the good society. They have demanded that their government take steps to mitigate the more pernicious by-products of the free market; they have insisted that education should be made universally available, free of charge; and they have urged that public funds be used to sustain them and assist them when they fall prey to inescapable hardships of life. Some of these new-found functions of government have unquestionably been provincial responsibilities, while others have required action at all three levels of government. But, in general, the burden of the new activities has been, and in all probability will continue to be, placed on the shoulders of the governments of the provinces.

This has meant a phenomenal increase in the functions of the Ontario Government. Let me illustrate this by reference to just two areas of provincial responsibility: education and social welfare.

In the first thirty-two years of the province's history less than $18 million was spent on education; today the Department of Education alone spends half a *billion* a year. In this century expenditures on education have increased from less than $2 per capita to over $60 per capita.

The field of social welfare, including health services, has undergone a transformation even more remarkable than has been the case in education. At the time of Confederation the care of the sick and the destitute was considered to be a private responsibility and the government's role was generally restricted to making grants to hospitals, orphans' homes, asylums and other charities. The total amount expended by the province of Ontario on social welfare in the last third of the nineteenth century was approximately $3.5 million. Today the province spends more than that amount for this purpose each week!

These two areas of increased government involvement have been singled out because they directly reflect the changes that have taken place in the attitudes of Canadians towards the state and because the growth of government in these fields has had a fundamental effect on the Canadian federal balance. However, all aspects of provincial government concern have expanded. A glance at the province's budgets in the last twenty-five years tells the story.

Looked at in terms of unadjusted dollars, the Ontario Government's net current and capital expenditures have increased at such an accelerated rate since 1945 as to make any comparisons with expenditures in the nineteenth century simply ludicrous. For example, if no allowance is made for changes in the value of the dollar, it may be said that government now spends in each *day* over twice as much as the total government expenditures in the whole first *year* of the province's existence.

So far as the overall trend is concerned, it may be said that up to about 1930 the federal government's share of total government expenditures tended to decline in proportion to the expenditures of the junior governments. Then, the chaos of the thirties and the requirements of war in the first half of the forties reversed the trend so that by the end of the war the federal government was spending three times as much as the provincial and municipal governments combined. However, with the return to normalcy in 1946, federalization of revenues and expenditures began again until, by the sixties, provincial and local governments together were spending more than the central government.

The implications of these trends for the politics of Canadian federalism are of fundamental significance but are beyond the scope of this paper. However, I would like to discuss to what extent our provincial institutions have been modified to cope with the new situation.

The executive branch has always been the most responsive to the pressures to adapt to the changing needs of the Ontario society. Perhaps the most elementary indication of this has been the steady growth in the size of the executive in Ontario.

The Cabinet itself, which was originally limited to five members, had grown to twenty-two members by 1960. But the growth in the size of the administrative arm of the executive has been much more rapid. In the early years of the province's history the Ontario public service consisted of a few hundred men and women, usually hand-picked by a government grateful for electoral support. By the turn of the century it still numbered only about seven hundred. This was only about seven civil servants for each MPP, so that it was relatively easy for the Legislature to keep tabs on the administration. Even the Premier knew most of the government's employees and was approached directly for jobs. (The classic illustration of this is the story of Sir J.P. Whitney. Sir James made a habit of riding a bike to his office and one morning he was overtaken by a man who informed him that the Sheriff of Manitoulin Island had died and then asked if he could take the Sheriff's place. The unperturbed Premier replied that it was all right with him if the undertaker didn't mind.) Since then the public service has continued to increase—even in the thirties, despite Mitch Hepburn's shenanigans—to approximately fifty thousand today.

Along with the growth in the size of the executive branch of government there has been a corresponding increase in the use of various executive instruments.

One of the most direct means available to the executive for giving effect to its will is the Order in Council. From the very beginning Orders in Council have been more numerous than the statutes by which they were authorized but they have increased in number far more rapidly than have the provincial statutes by which they are authorized and now number over five thousand per year, compared to fewer than two hundred statutes passed by the Legislative Assembly.

The executive may also make use of Special Warrants and Treasury Board Orders to accomplish its purpose if the appropriations voted by the Legislative Assembly should ever prove inadequate. In spite of the fact that the Estimates usually exceed actual expenditures by about 8 percent each year, the Government still finds it necessary to create and spend new appropriations by means of Special Warrants and Treasury Board Orders.

Besides simply expanding and making more use of executive instruments, the executive branch has been reorganized and made efficient. Again, most of these changes have been made since the end of the Second World War.

As late as 1946, when Roland Michener became Provincial Secretary in the Drew ministry, the Cabinet lacked even the most rudimentary organization. There was no agenda for Cabinet meetings. The only record of what was done in the meetings consisted of the Orders in Council which were passed. Committees were used only infrequently and then on a strictly ad hoc basis. There was no secretary of the Cabinet except the Provincial Secretary himself.

Mr. Michener and his assistant, Lorne McDonald, studied procedures used at Westminster and Ottawa and began to adapt them to the

136

needs of the Ontario Cabinet. Agendas were prepared and informal minutes were kept. When Mr. Michener lost his seat in the 1948 election, Mr. McDonald was appointed the first Secretary of the Cabinet from outside the Executive Council itself. Today the Secretary of the Cabinet has a staff of over twenty-five to assist him.

Committees became an integral part of Cabinet organization in the late forties and early fifties under the premiership of Leslie Frost.

There is one other significant way in which the executive branch has been modified in order to cope with the increased responsibilities of government. In keeping with the pattern in most modern democracies, the Ontario Government has not only enlarged and modified the older elements in the executive branch but has created new bodies that operate outside of the traditional framework of the Cabinet and the civil service. I am referring here to the one hundred odd boards and commissions that are currently in existence.

The whole problem of the relationship between these relatively recent accretions to the administrative machinery of the state and the older institutions of government is still very much an open question. Because they have resulted from our failure to adapt our traditional liberal democratic institutions to the demands of the positive state in a collectivist society, they have been very difficult to integrate into the overall system.

The aim of liberal democratic theory was the maximization of individual freedom—conceived as the absence of restraint—and the separation of powers was the means to that end. By setting up institutions to check the executive and by giving those institutions powers suited to their task, they sought to divide and so to limit the overall power of the state. Institutions devised to put into practice such a limited concept of the legitimate role of the state were hardly suitable for governing a social welfare state. So, rather than attempt to use these institutions for an assignment for which they were not intended, the usual tendency has been to graft on to them new institutions more suited to the task.

It comes as no surprise to note that, almost invariably, these new institutions violate the principle of the separation of powers in that a given agency will usually perform legislative and executive—and sometimes judicial—functions, often without any system of appeal to the major legislative, executive, or judicial institutions of government.

In Ontario, classical liberal shibboleths still command apparent, if

137

not actual, acceptance. Thus, the Government—wanting to maintain a facade of limited government and yet compelled to intervene in more and more areas of public concern in order to survive—has resorted to extra-departmental agencies as a compromise solution to their dilemma. This expediency salves their own liberal consciences and also meets the demands of the organized pressure groups who want the kind of control over their operations that can be achieved only through public authority but who nevertheless fear direct government supervision of their activities—no doubt because they too were nurtured on the principles of laissez-faire liberalism. It seems the province suffers from philosophical schizophrenia: compelled to preach old-fashioned liberalism but forced to practice something quite different.

I will return to this theme later, but before leaving the executive I would like to mention one major area where the Ontario Cabinet has yet to modernize. Modern behavioural research has created some powerful tools to assist in policy formulation but, to date, the Provincial Government has not availed itself of them, proceeding instead on the old trial and error method. As usual, the Federal Government is ahead of us here. Indeed many of the facts and figures that *are* used by the Provincial Government are provided by the Federal Government. Not only has Ottawa got fact-finding agencies like the Dominion Bureau of Statistics but Mr. Trudeau has created a powerful policy group in his own office which, in turn, can use the information provided by the forty-five task forces presently at work—most of which are using modern research methods.

Nevertheless, the executive branch in Ontario has progressed much further and much faster than the legislative branch.

Starting again with the most obvious point of comparison, it may be said that the size of the Legislative Assembly has not increased significantly. Currently it consists of 117 members, compared to 82 in 1867. It may very well be that increasing the size of the legislature would not improve its position vis-a-vis the executive but there is still some significance to the fact that, whereas the Cabinet accounted for only 6 percent of the membership of the House in 1867, it included over 22 percent of the House in 1960. Furthermore, the Cabinet has on occasion included nearly a third of the members belonging to the governing party.

The static nature of the legislative branch is also illustrated by the fact that the sessions of the Legislature have not lengthened appreciably over the years. In the decade following the war, when govern-ment activity was expanding apace, the sessions averaged 45.5 days, one day *less* than the average length of the province's *first* ten sessions.

Again, while the executive branch has experimented with new organizations and developed modern procedures, the Legislative Assembly has continued to labour under essentially the same pro-cedure that it copied from its colonial predecessor in 1867. The writ-ten rules have never been altered fundamentally and they have not been amended at all since 1939. Changes have been made by custom but, on balance, these have been to the benefit of the members of the executive rather than the private members.

For example, the written rules stipulate that all items shall be taken up according to the precedence assigned to each on the Order paper, except that the administration is permitted to call Govern-ment orders in whatever order they see fit on those days when Govern-ment bills have precedence, namely Tuesdays and Thursdays. The rules notwithstanding, the custom of the House is for the Premier to call *all* orders without regard to the precedence assigned to them. Until 1966 this meant that there was no time when private members' business automatically had precedence and no private member's legislation was debated unless the Premier allowed it. Now two hours a week are set aside, but about half of this time is reserved for members of the governing party.

In the light of the size and complexity of modern government, perhaps the basic pre-condition of an efficient legislature is adequate information. No matter what role is ascribed to the legislative branch—and no particular role has thus far been suggested here—the degree of success it achieves will in all likelihood depend to' a large extent upon its accessibility to the information it requires. Unfortunately, this is one of those areas which have seen little improvement in Ontario.

So far as the formal institutions of government are concerned, the most convenient method of gaining information is the parliamentary question and, since the situation with regard to questions in Ontario is fairly typical of other methods of eliciting information from the Government, I will focus on this one aspect of the larger problem.

There are two types of questions used in the Ontario Legislature. First, there is the written question which must be handed in to the

Clerk before five o'clock on any day in order to appear on the Order Paper two days later. When the answer is ready—and when the Prime Minister wants to give it—he will simply table it and it will be printed in *Hansard*. He does not read the answer, as is done with "starred" questions at Ottawa and Westminster, and therefore there can be no oral supplementary questions. But even worse is the fact that the Government takes so long to reply. In Britain, all questions are answered within three days; in Ontario, in the four month session of 1964, for example, the Government took an average of forty-eight days to answer our members' questions. (And this in spite of the fact that in the years I have looked at, an average of only twenty-five questions were asked in Ontario compared to an average of over twelve thousand in the United Kingdom.)

Secondly, there is the oral question before the Orders of the Day. Notice must be given to the Speaker before twelve o'clock on the day that the question is to be asked and he can refuse questions which do not seem to him to be urgent. There is nothing like the practice at Ottawa where questions may be asked of Ministers without any notice whatsoever. The members of the Ontario Cabinet are never confronted with parliamentary questions of which they and their civil servants have had no previous knowledge. As it is, the question period, which Jennings called the "cocktails before the oratorical feast", is more like cold leftovers.

On the basis of this evidence it may be concluded that members do not find parliamentary questions to be useful tools for acquiring their much needed information. Of little more usefulness are the various publications of the Government. However, in recent years select committees have become potentially valuable instruments for informing the members about various topics of government responsibility. They are, of course, dominated by the party in power but they do provide opportunities for members to do some investigation of their own.

This leads to another aspect of the private member's situation that deserves attention, namely the lack of adequate facilities and staff for MPPs. Until the 1965 session there was practically no office space whatsoever available for private members. Now each member has his own desk and telephone, but they still labour under conditions that must make serious work all but impossible.

Secretarial staff has been made available to the opposition parties only since 1956 and, together with the extra stenographic assistance provided during the session, it is probably adequate for routine work. But no money was made available for research staff until 1965 and the current grant for this purpose is inadequate to even begin doing the job that needs to be done. The staff of the Legislative Library is not able to do research for members.

One other indication of the plight of the legislative branch needs to be mentioned. While the executive has increased its use of various executive instruments, there has been no change in legislative procedure to provide for the review of the executive's use of these instruments. There is no scrutiny committee, no provision for tabling Orders in Council or other types of subordinate legislation, and no specific opportunities for members to discuss these items in the House. In the case of the semi-independent agencies the situation is even less satisfactory. In most cases, the Legislature has delegated powers to the agencies without at the same time providing for any means of exercising any control over the use of the powers so delegated.

When pressure is put upon the Government to make provision for procedures whereby the Legislature could maintain some control over its delegated powers, its standard reply is that the principle of ministerial responsibility is an adequate safeguard against abuse. But it is doubtful if the concept of ministerial responsibility has any relevance in Ontario's system of disciplined one-party dominance.

As far as individual ministerial responsibility is concerned, the fact of the matter is that so long as a minister has the confidence of the Prime Minister his position is secure. The Government simply accepts responsibility for his actions and he falls under the protective cloak of collective responsibility. And collective responsibility has little more meaning. It is no great concession for a government to accept responsibility for its deeds when neither Parliament nor the public have access to the information needed to call it to account— and when it has a solid majority behind it in case they do. If Ontario ever elected a minority government, the principle of ministerial responsibility would have some utility. But, with such large majorities (averaging 70 percent of the seats in the current period of Conservative party dominance) it means nothing more than that ministers cannot publicly disagree with their colleagues. And on occasion even this happens.

The tendency to concentrate power in the hands of the executive while at the same time denying the legislative branch the means of controlling the use of this power poses a problem of fundamental importance to anyone committed to the preservation of some form of democracy. James Mill noted that "all the difficult questions of government relate to the means of restraining those, in whose hands are lodged the powers for the protection of all, from making a bad use of it", and Justice Frankfurter was right when he said, "The history of liberty has largely been the history of the observance of procedural safeguards." Under constitutions of the parliamentary variety, the institution charged with primary responsibility for this task has traditionally been the legislature and, more particularly, the Opposition. So far as the formal, visible institutions of government are concerned, the government backbencher is little more than a cipher. As Sir Ivor Jennings put it, "The Government's majority exists to support the Government."

Thus, when we consider the role of the Opposition in Ontario, we are not toying with the fringes of the political process but are probing the very essence of parliamentary, democratic government, albeit in microcosm. Indeed, if Carl Friedrich is right in equating constitution-alism with the separation of powers within the state, we are ultimately concerned here with the nature of constitutionalism in a system of government resting on the principle of the fusion of legislative and executive powers. If any governmental institution is given specific responsibility for checking the executive in Ontario, it is the Opposi-tion and, unless sufficient power is given to the Opposition to enable it to perform this function, institutional democracy at the provincial level of government is in jeopardy.

Thus, what is needed in the years that lie ahead in Ontario is an efficient Cabinet that will use all of the resources it can muster to determine the needs and aspirations of the citizens and then devise imaginative policies to meet them. But, at the same time great care must be taken to ensure that our elected representatives, of whatever party, are provided the means for *keeping* that Cabinet responsible to the people.

20

The Liberal Plan for Responsible Government
Vernon Singer

There has been a lot of public comment lately to the effect that all is not well at Queen's Park, that perhaps democracy is ailing, that our system is bad, that the "bad guys" are in charge and things would be immeasurably better if we, "the good guys", took over.

But with all this talk, why, really, do we participate in politics? Why do we spend time, money, and effort putting on conferences? For some these meetings are pleasant social gatherings. For some with a political disease in our blood, anything that can be done to help throw the rascals out is a worthwhile exercise. For some there is a genuine hope that we can improve the Ontario environment and can produce a better life for *all* of our citizens.

Are things really that bad in Ontario? After all, today most people are living better than ever before. We are better housed, clothed, fed, paid, educated and looked after by government than any other group of people in the history of mankind. We have medicare, unemployment insurance, hospital services, old age pensions, accessible and good educational services, high taxes (but money to pay them), comparative freedom of speech and religion, the right to dissent, legal aid, anti-discrimination laws. We have good roads but bad public transportation, minimal unemployment, free press, leisure time, libraries, swimming pools, parks, a pretty good system for the administration of justice with reasonably competent police forces. We can go south in the winter and north in the summer. Our teen agers (though somewhat restless) are the best looked after in the history of the world. Thousands can even travel abroad long before they have completed their education or begun to earn a living. Some can even call the Prime Minister of Canada obscene names and get away with it.

I have painted a pretty picture of a successful and prosperous society, but more careful examination must lead us to the conclusion that a large segment of the population is denied the benefits of this "place to stand and a place to grow"! Many people, and their children, suffer grave inequities through no fault of their own. The state is really not discharging its obligations to *all* its citizens. And so we are concerned.

We believe our form of government can be better—more caring, less arrogant and intolerant, *that all people should be able to benefit from our affluent society*, that we should be planning now for the problems of the next thirty years! It is not enough to say that Robert F. Nixon is better than John P. Robarts (though he is)—that the Liberal team is more aware, more concerned and competent than that same old gang of Tories who have been there for twenty-six years. Nor can we afford to hand over all our government institutions to a group of socialist idealists who believe they know better than anyone else and that the true panacea for all our ills is to wage the class war and insert government control (their control) into every facet of our lives.

We are also deeply concerned about our parliamentary processes. We are sick to death of the traditional proceedings, nurtured and kept alive by overbearing government, majorities—proceedings that deny elected representatives an opportunity to inquire into and help shape the path of government action. Our old-fashioned rules deny us the right to speak when we should, to get information we feel we are entitled to, to bring to a vote issues which are not government selected. All these and many more are evils that have to be eradicated.

Aided and abetted by the press, or perhaps even being led by them, we politicians have been able to convince the public that we are really an incompetent lot. We continue to follow ancient procedures in the conduct of our legislative business. Could anything be more ridiculous than the ritual rain dances in which we indulge, officially known as the Budget Debates. The Government introduces the budget after hiding all advance copies under a tight security screen (complete with OPP guards) until it is actually revealed in the Legislature.

The press, in the meantime, has had several hours to analyze and write stories before the presentation is even complete. Opposition leaders are expected to present an instant and intelligent criticism. Lord forbid anyone in Opposition should break their rule at this point and say, "It's a good budget!" It must be referred to as a "Doomsday budget", a "flip-flop budget" and so on.

The same problem occurs with a new piece of legislation. Moments after it is introduced (and certainly long before the Opposition has had a chance to examine it) the press again wants, and most frequently gets, instant opinions on what may be a brand new theory of government.

Even a few nights ago, when Prime Minister Trudeau was announcing his austerity guidelines (and I would guess that neither Mr. Stanfield nor Mr. Douglas were provided with advance copies), the media were asking for, and getting, standard, hackneyed criticism from these gentlemen. Could they reasonably criticize this most important piece of Government policy, having only just heard about it: a program that the Government spent weeks or months preparing, that an army of civil servants was able to research and analyze in advance? Even if the policy were acceptable, perish the thought that they would be able to find any good in Trudeau's announcement—that just isn't the way the game is played. They must provide *instant* criticism!

Yes, politicians are a bad lot. Some of us even say that about ourselves. Perhaps you saw a quotation attributed to a Toronto school trustee (the same one who recently was criticized for a trip to Hawaii, at public expense, for a music convention to which Canadians had not even been invited). This particular politician was against the suggestion of handing over some control of the Board of Education budget to the Council of the City of Toronto because he felt they were "political hacks"!

It has become the popular thing to deride politics and sneer at our politicians. Everyone looks for the "statesman", whatever that word might mean. (Someone once described a statesman as a dead politician.) However, the fact remains that the art of politics is a most vital one, which, when properly practiced, I believe will preserve our democratic form of government. Politicians are as good or as bad as their electors allow them to be. Our form of government allows us change on all levels when we are dissatisfied with our elected representatives.

Therefore, if we believe that the democratic system of government is worth preserving, we hurt only ourselves when we deride as a "political" decision or manoeuvre, any course of action of which we do not approve. All decisions affecting the body politic are "political" decisions, whether they relate to the construction of a sewer, the use of the strap in our schools, the recognition of Red China or the

145

appointment of an assessor for the County of Middlesex. The persons who make these decisions are politicians. Surely, it is important that all of us, rather than tear down by glib criticism when we disagree with a particular political decision, constructively direct our criticism to seeking remedies. Loose talking and thinking does nothing more than make it harder every day to continue the democratic process in the way we would like to see it continue; makes it harder to attract competent, devoted and intelligent people to serve in the government on all levels.

How often (if ever) do you hear any government spokesman, no matter how wrong he may have been, admit that he has made an error? I am sure the people of Ontario would appreciate a government spokesman who, once in a while when an ill-conceived piece of legislation has been introduced, would admit that Opposition criticism had been helpful and intelligent. After all, what all of us are really trying to do is to pass better legislation!

But, again, this is not the way the game is played. Even when the error has become so patently obvious that it must be rectified, it is most often accompanied by some mealy-mouthed explanation of rectitude; or slipped in, apparently unobtrusively, at a much later date. This is then designated as a further example of the continuing brilliance of those who inhabit the seats of the mighty.

The complaint from citizens that they are not consulted on decisions which affect them personally, is a justified one. Their property may be expropriated and they cannot argue. They are subject to the rule of nameless and faceless civil servants. This often results in the demand for citizen participation in decision making.

There was even the ridiculous suggestion made recently by a professor of Economics that aldermen should, in advance of starting their elected duties, hand a resignation in blank and assignment of their pay to the ratepayers' president. This would guarantee the good behaviour of the aldermen (living up to their election promises, I guess) and would ensure that the president could keep the aldermen under control. The learned professor failed to explain: Who chooses the ratepayers' president?

We *must* modernize our parliamentary procedures so that the whole apparatus is no longer a shield to protect the cabinet from the members, particularly Opposition members. It must be clearly established that there is a right to inquire and a right to get answers. (Not as Allan Lawrence, the present Minister of Mines, alleges, "The Opposition has no right to know!") Let those persons who are elected to public office recognize that their electors are not stupid; that no one is really impressed with the statement that public affairs must be conducted in keeping with fixed patterns "because they have always been conducted in this way". When change is required, change will be made!

Those who seek and are chosen for public office are expected by their constituents to have opinions and to express them, and to have the right to express them. All members of the Legislature, be they Cabinet Ministers or members of the Opposition or even Government backbenchers, have the right and duty to express their opinion, even when those opinions might differ with those of the party leader.

I believe that voters really do not care whether the Legislature sits in session 365 days a year and 24 hours a day, as long as the public business is suitably looked after. The voters are not really impressed by the vicious insult hurled at an opponent, nor by the often too clever use of obscure procedural rules, to stifle reasonable discussion of a particular subject. From time to time, there is nothing either degrading or harmful in admitting that a mistake has been made, and in taking proper action to correct it. The voters do, however, expect all their elected representatives to participate intelligently and mean-ingfully in the decisions which affect the Province of Ontario.

Departments of government must be restructured to fit into today's society. We have no need of twenty-three cabinet ministers, under old titles and old divisions. This only produces confusion, denies information, and makes consistent planning impossible. There is no good reason for keeping highways and transport separated into two departments. They should be joined into one. What use is the Provincial Secretary? Surely all matters relating to parks (and there are about eight departments of government now looking after various aspects) could be in the same department! The same can be said about a department of urban affairs. In all, we plan to reduce the number of departments to fifteen.

A citizen who is abused by a civil servant should be able to complain to an independent ombudsman, appointed by Parliament as a whole, not by the government in power. The ombudsman is a servant of the people, empowered to see files, call witnesses and fight the citizens' fight against the anonymous civil servants.

The Opposition critic for, say, the Department of Health, must criticize a minister who has 20,000 civil servants, secretaries, executive assistants, research facilities and public money to hire new people for specific projects. The Opposition members have almost none of these resources! The people of Ontario are not being well served by their members because they have neither the facilities to criticize constructively in the Legislature, nor those to explore properly the legitimate, often personal concerns of his individual constituent. All members, and particularly members of the Opposition, must be given proper facilities to do their job. They need private offices, secretarial help, research help and riding help. The job of an MPP is now a full-time job; to serve his constituency properly and to make a reasonable contribution in the Legislature, he needs to be prepared.

If someone is in need of assistance in housing, he now goes to the Ontario Housing Corporation. In many instances the need for housing is only a symptom. The root of the problem may be illness, old age, marital trouble, alcoholism, lack of education, trouble with the law, or any combination of these. Ontario Housing deals only with housing and gives advice only on this aspect. Advice on other problems must be made available to all citizens. We must establish government offices throughout Ontario to provide advice about and assistance in obtaining all the government services which an individual may need when he has a problem.

There should be a greater opportunity for citizen participation in decision making. This can be done in part by the expansion and meaningful use of select committees. These committees would sit year round and would not convene just at the behest of the government for limited purpose, such as consideration of a statute. The committees would not be controlled absolutely by a government majority. Opposition members might be allowed to chair some of them. They should be empowered to summon witnesses, produce documents, hold hearings in public. Concerned groups of citizens would be permitted to make representations to these all-party committees, not just to cabinet ministers. I do not suggest leaving the actual decisions to non-elected persons; but I do want to provide for consultation with concerned and knowledgeable people. The elected representatives, who must answer to the electors, must retain the final responsibility for decision making.

Civilian control of police forces is a must! I would hope that committees of the local council could do the job. The provincial courts and small claims courts must be improved. A personal visit to these courts is necessary to comprehend fully how degrading an experience it is for all who participate in proceedings there. They take place in dingy, dirty, airless rooms, court clerks shout rudely at everyone, they sit only for half-days, the procedures are poor. There are so many other things that should be provided like meaningful night courts, privacy laws, wiretap laws, bail reform. We hope to bring the Just Society to Ontario.

There is far too much waste today, and no real ability by the Legislature to control it. We must exercise real control of costs of government through proper business analyses. The best example of abuse today is the fantastic expenditure by boards of education. I have serious doubts about their continued effectiveness. We should create a common council where a committee of council is charged with the responsibility for education. We could then do away with boards of education. As we get more regional governments, it will result in more full time politicians, and, thus, better public control. We also need more democratic control over other spending bodies, such as Hydro, liquor boards, Public Utilities Commissions.

In conclusion, let me say that there is much to be done if we wish to reestablish responsible government in Ontario. The Liberal Party in Ontario is eager to accept the challenge.